MODERN
MATHEMATICIANS

MODERN MATHEMATICIANS

Harry Henderson

☑® Facts On File, Inc.

Modern Mathematicians

Library of Congress Cataloging-in-Publication Data

Henderson, Harry, 1951–
    Modern mathematicians / Harry Henderson.
        p. cm. — (Global profiles)
    Includes bibliographical references (p –) and index.
    ISBN 0-8160-3235-1 (hb : acid-free)
    1. Mathematicians—Biography. I. Title. II. Series.
QA28.H46 1996
510.92´2—dc20   95–18363
    [B]

Text design by Catherine Rincon Hyman
Cover design by Nora Wertz
Diagrams by Katherine Macfarlane

Front cover photographs:
Blackboard (© Steve Belkowitz/FPG International); Ada Lovelace (Hilton Deutsch Collection); Charles Babbage; Alan Turing (© Photographer, Science Source/Photo Researchers); Emmy Noether (Bryn Mawr College Archives); Srinivasa Ramanujan (Master and fellows of Trinity College, Cambridge).

This book is printed on acid-free paper.

Printed in the United States of America

MP FOF 10 9 8 7 6 5 4 3 2

To the young women and men

who will uncover

the next chapter of the

story of mathematics.

Contents

Acknowledgments

I would like to thank Katherine Macfarlane for turning my wiggly sketches into clear diagrams. Thanks also to Dr. Shiing-Shen Chern for gracious conversation and for filling in details about his life and work. As always, I appreciate the help of the staffs of the Richmond and Berkeley public libraries for reference help and for the invaluable Interlibrary Loan Service. I would also like to express my appreciation for help in obtaining photographs and other material to: Patricia Ardito and the American Mathematical Society, the Mathematical Association of America, and the Science Museum, Kensington, London.

Introduction

This book presents the lives of 13 people who made a variety of important contributions to modern mathematics. Mathematics has been called "the language of science" and "the queen of the sciences." Mathematics is so important to science because it gives people a way to systematically explore patterns and relationships.

At bottom, that's what mathematics is—patterns. If they are patterns of lines, circles, and shapes, we call it geometry. If they are patterns of known numbers we call it arithmetic. If some of the numbers are unknown, we can use algebra to find the missing part of the pattern. More advanced forms of mathematics deal with other kinds of patterns: calculus, for example, deals with the way changes in one quantity (force, for example) affect changes in another quantity (such as velocity). Since scientists are always seeking to understand patterns and relationships in the physical world, they use mathematics as a tool for probing nature and as a language for describing exactly what they have found.

The title of this book is *Modern Mathematicians* because the people in this book lived and worked in the last two centuries (three are still active today). It would take many more books like this one to survey all the remarkable lives and important achievements that make up modern mathematics. But the stories of the 13 mathematicians profiled in this book's 12 chapters will give you a good taste of the diversity of modern mathematics.

Our first pair of mathematicians, Charles Babbage and Ada Lovelace, worked in the first half of the 19th century. This was a time when the Industrial Revolution was reaching full stride. A growing industrial economy needed detailed mathematical tables so people could calculate bank interest, write insurance policies, and design better steam engines. Babbage and Lovelace, seeing how machines were starting to transform their world, dreamed of a machine that could weave numbers like the steam loom wove cloth. Though a practical computer was just beyond their grasp, their heirs in the 20th century would take up the challenge.

Alan Turing designed a theoretical "universal computer" that could perform complex calculations using the simplest possible steps. When World War II came, he designed a real computer that broke a complex German cipher and helped win the war for the Allies. He later sketched out chess-playing programs and looked ahead to a time when computers might be able to think in the same ways that people do.

Stanislaw Ulam helped design atomic and hydrogen bombs for a war that thankfully never happened. But more important, he showed how the computer could do more than calculate rapidly. What scientists could not calculate, Ulam found, a computer could be made to simulate by "rolling the dice" electronically. Today some computer simulations educate and entertain us while others make it possible to design complex machines such as the space shuttle.

John Conway showed that serious mathematics could be done through fun and games. Building on the work of Ulam and John von Neumann, Conway developed "games" that showed how systems made of many simple parts could create amazingly lifelike phenomena such as motion, reproduction, and growth. You can play Conway's Game of Life on your home computer.

While these mathematicians were revolutionizing computing, others were looking deeply into the nature of number itself. In the 19th century, George Boole designed the true/false 1/0 logic that underlies today's computer circuits. He also devised the now familiar set theory that showed how things could be classified and compared in new ways.

Georg Cantor extended the idea of sets to look at how numbers themselves made up different kinds of sets—including infinite sets that, though unending, could still be compared to one another. Cantor's surprising conclusion was that some infinities are more infinite than others.

If Cantor was the classical virtuoso of numbers, Srinivasa Ramanujan was one of mathematics' greatest jazz artists. In the early 20th century Europeans still tended to think of mathematics as being their exclusive property. They were thus astonished when an unknown young man from India improvised an endless stream of subtle and powerful formulas. Ramanujan proved that, in David Hilbert's words: "Mathematics knows no races . . . for mathematics, the whole cultural world is a single country." After his tragically short life had ended, mathematicians continued to delve into Ramanujan's notebooks in search of mathematical truth.

Ramanujan had begun to make modern mathematics truly international, but it remained a male-dominated profession. Carl Friedrich Gauss, writing to Sophie Germain (a pioneer female mathematician) at the beginning of the 19th century, had noted that "when a person of the sex, which according to our customs and prejudices, must encounter infinitely more difficulties than men, to familiarize herself with these thorny researches, succeeds nevertheless in surmounting these obstacles and penetrating the most obscure parts of them, then without doubt she must have the noblest courage, quite extraordinary talents and a superior genius."

We will never know how many women of past centuries might have become Newtons or Einsteins if they had only been given the chance. When Ada Lovelace, bound by the social customs of her time, nevertheless helped Charles Babbage develop and publicize his computer ideas, she could list only her initials on her writings.

But about 50 years later, Sofia Kovalevskaia, who surely had all of the qualities Gauss had mentioned, succeeded in demonstrating that women could reach the very first rank of mathematical achievement. Kovalevskaia's creativity and perseverance overcame every barrier put before her by a 19th century university system that barred women students. She found the teachers she needed and then created equations that would help solve the mystery of Saturn's rings. Her work won her the prestigious Bordin Prize. She went on to become the first tenured woman university professor in modern Europe.

In the early 20th century, when barriers against women mathematicians were only slightly less high, Emmy Noether became the queen of abstract algebra while defying the Nazis. In our own times, Julia Robinson faced less determined opposition when she sought a career in mathematics—though the "ordinary" difficulties were hard enough. She, too, persevered, and solved one of the great unsolved problems of number theory.

The works of these 13 mathematicians were accomplished in a changing scientific world. These changes have had two major themes. The first is the way that the abstract ideas of mathematics have often turned out to provide the tools needed by scientists who were seeking a deeper understanding of the physical world. For example, Emmy Noether's work on groups (an elaboration of sets) and their operations brought her into close partnership with the quantum physicists who were seeking a theory that would explain the behavior of sub-atomic particles.

The new geometries of curved spaces that seemed to be just a mathematical curiosity in the late 19th century turned out to be necessary for describing the world of Einstein's theory of relativity. In the universe of relativity, space is curved, not straight or flat. Later in this century, Shiing-Shen Chern would revitalize geometry and discover a model of "fiber bundle" space that is now being used by physicists who are trying to map the fundamental forces of the universe (gravity, electromagnetism, and the strong and weak nuclear forces) in a web of many dimensions.

A second theme of modern mathematics (particularly in the 20th century) is the change in the way mathematicians have looked at their subject. The ancient Greek mathematicians (such as Euclid) saw mathematics as revealing unchanging truth. Plato declared that "the knowledge at which geometry aims is the knowledge of the eternal." As late as this century, the great British mathematician G. H. Hardy insisted that: "317 is a prime, not because we think so, or because our minds are shaped in one way rather than another, but *because it is so*, because mathematical reality is built that way."

But what *is* mathematical reality? In the 1930s Kurt Gödel and Alan Turing showed in different ways that mathematics will always ask some questions that it can't answer. (At about the same time physicist Werner Heisenberg formulated his Uncertainty Principle, which stated the limits on what an observer can learn about a particle). The quest for truth did not end with the acceptance of uncertainty, but the rules of the game had changed. Mathematics does continue to reveal beautiful patterns and even truths of universal validity, but part of that truth is found in things that seem to be "messy" or chaotic.

Indeed, chaos turned out to have a remarkable beauty of its own. As Benoit Mandelbrot began to look at seemingly random bits of data, he discovered layers of patterns in the way the bits clumped together. This formed the basis of fractal geometry, which can be used to generate striking patterns on a computer screen, but also to study questions in economics, weather forecasting, biology, and other fields. We are just beginning to discover the possible applications of the new "science of chaos."

You are living at a particularly good time for mathematical discovery. The availability of powerful, inexpensive computers gives you tools that go far beyond the notebooks and blackboards used by earlier mathematicians. The attitudes that sometimes discouraged young would-be mathematicians are changing. High school teacher Jaime Escalante (whose story is told in the movie *Stand and Deliver*) led his inner-city students to a mastery of college-level calculus. A special effort is being made by groups such as EQUALS to help girls discover and express their talent for mathematics. Mathematics has always been diverse in its ideas, but now the world of mathematicians is beginning to show cultural diversity.

The growing world-wide computer networks bring together teachers and students on every continent. A discovery made in a laboratory in London can be used the next day by a researcher in Nairobi, Kenya. If a book like this is written during the 21st century, it will no doubt include great mathematicians, both men and women, from Africa and Latin America as well as Europe, America, and Asia.

MODERN
MATHEMATICIANS

Charles Babbage, living in the Age of Steam, designed a computer remarkably like those used today. (Science & Society Picture Library)

Charles Babbage

(1792–1871) and

Ada Lovelace

(1815–1852)

By the 1850s, the growth of industry and the development of new technology had created a world that would have been unthinkable only half a century earlier. Steam-powered factories sawed lumber and wove cloth. Steam also propelled ships across the ocean and railroad trains across a growing network in America and Europe. This new industrial world was tied together by the telegraph, which harnessed electricity to send messages hundreds of miles in an instant. In little more than a generation talented scientists and inventors had made amazing breakthroughs in manufacturing, transportation, and communication. But one important task, calculation, was still done by hand: slowly, painstakingly, and with frequent errors.

But suppose one more invention had been made. Imagine steam-driven computers filled with thousands of gears. As the gears whirl, long numbers are added or subtracted in the blink of an eye and without error. The results would make it easier for banks, insurance companies, and governments to manage their affairs. Aided by such computers, scientists might have made today's discoveries a century sooner.

In reality, practical, general-purpose computers were not invented until the 1940s. But if two remarkable pioneeers, Charles Babbage and Ada Lovelace, had succeeded in turning their ideas into reality, the Information Age might have dawned 150 year ago. Our grandparents might have played computer games or even listened to music composed by computer.

Charles Babbage was born in London on the day after Christmas, 1791. His family belonged to the new class of successful business people who were starting to replace the old aristocracy as the "movers and shakers" of British society.

As a young boy, Charles was fascinated by mechanical toys. He was not satisfied until he knew every secret of their construction, even if he had to break them open to get at their parts. His other chief interest, seemingly opposite to the solid reality of mechanical gadgets, was the supernatural world of ghosts and spirits. Perhaps this interest started when Charles, at the age of five, became very sick and almost died.

As a teenager, Charles went to a boarding school near his home. He did well in his studies and was especially fascinated by mathematics. He found a few algebra books in the school's small library and decided that he wanted to learn their secrets.

The school didn't offer a class in algebra, but Charles didn't let that stop him. He found another boy who also liked to study. They decided to get up together each morning at 3 A.M. The two boys went to the library, lit a fire to keep warm, and studied until about 5:30. As other boys found out about their improvised "night school," they joined in. Sometimes the study session turned into a party. After several months, the noise from the library grew loud enough to attract the attention of the school authorities, who chased the boys back to bed.

By the time he entered Trinity College, Cambridge, in 1810, Babbage had studied algebra and calculus thoroughly, both with a tutor and by himself. He became familiar with the works of the great European mathematicians of the time. After he read a book called *Differential and Integral Calculus* by the French mathematician S. F. Lacroix, he joined together with John Herschel and George Peacock to form the Analytical Society. (Calculus is the branch of mathematics that deals with how quantities change in relation to one another.)

The goal of this group was to replace the kind of calculus that had been invented about 150 years earlier by Isaac Newton with new European methods that Babbage and his friends felt were more flexible and powerful. Conservative members of the university faculty ridiculed the society's efforts. Because Newton had used dots to show derivatives of a variable while the Europeans used the letter d (as in dx/dy), instead, the Analytical Society published a volume of papers with the title *The Principles of Pure D-ism in opposition to the Dot-age of the University.* The title contained two puns: "D-ism" could be spelled Deism (a popular religious doctrine of the time), while "dotage" meant the feeblemindedness and rigidity sometimes found in old people.

By the age of 25, Babbage had already achieved a great deal. Together with Herschel and Peacock, he published an English translation of Lacroix's book. He also wrote three papers of his own on calculus. In 1815, Babbage was elected a Fellow of the British Royal Society, the nation's most famous scientific organization.

But Babbage was beginning to turn his attention from math theory to a pressing practical problem. In the early

1800s, tables of logarithms, angles, probabilities, and other mathematical functions were becoming increasingly important in everyday life. The navy, which was responsible for patrolling a worldwide British Empire, needed accurate navigation tables. Insurance companies needed statistics that could tell them what the risk of death for a person of a certain age would be. Bankers needed tables of interest rates, and engineers needed to calculate strengths of materials and steam pressures. All of these tables had to be painstakingly calculated by hand. This took thousands of hours of work by mathematicians and skilled clerks.

When Babbage looked over some printed tables, he discovered that despite the best efforts of human calculators, they were riddled with errors. One day, while reading a table of logarithms (powers of 10), Babbage fell asleep. Another friend walked in and said to him, "Well, Babbage, what are you dreaming about?" "I am thinking that all these tables might be calculated by machines," Babbage answered. He had come up with the idea of automatic calculation. If machines in factories could automatically weave patterns of cloth, he thought, a machine might be able to "weave" numbers and calculate whatever tables people needed, swiftly and without error. The quest for a practical computer would consume much of the rest of Babbage's working life.

Between 1820 and 1822, Babbage built a mechanical calculator that he called a difference engine. It relied on the fact that many mathematical functions could be calculated using only differences (subtractions) followed by appropriate additions. The small demonstration model of the difference engine worked well, but it was limited to producing short numbers with six to eight figures. Babbage decided to build a more powerful calculator, "Difference Engine Number One." This machine would have about 25,000 moving parts, could handle up to 20 decimal places, and

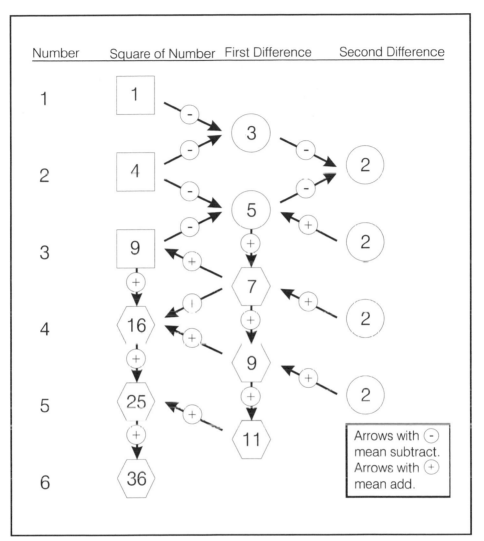

The method of differences used by the difference engine. To generate a table of squares, the machine starts with 1, 2, 3, and their squares 1, 4, and 9. The pairs of squares are subtracted from one another to get the first differences (in circles). The first differences are then subtracted from each other to get second differences (also in circles). Next, each second difference and the previous first difference are added together to get a new first difference (in hexagons). Finally, each first difference and the previous square are added together to get a new square for the table (in hexagons).

(Courtesy of Katherine Macfarlane)

would even have a printer that would print the results directly into tables, avoiding transcription errors.

Babbage thought that Difference Engine Number One could be built in only a few years, but he encountered endless difficulties. Just figuring out the effects of friction, tension, and "backlash" among thousands of gears turned out to be an engineer's nightmare. Workmen weren't used to building parts that required such precise measurement, and they had to invent new tools and techniques as they went along. By 1830, Babbage had matched contributions from the government with large amounts of his own money, but the machine was still far from complete. A dispute arose in 1833 about whether the workers were to move to new workshops built at Babbage's home. Gradually the project ground to a halt, and Difference Engine Number One remained unfinished.

By then, however, Babbage's thoughts had turned in a new direction. In 1836, he wrote in his notebook:

> This day I had for the first time a general but very indistinct conception of making an engine work out *algebraic* developments—I mean without any reference to the *value* of the letters [symbols]. My notion is that the cards (Jacquards) of the calc. engine direct a series of operations and then recommence [begin again] with the first, so that it might be possible to cause the same cards to punch others equivalent to any number of repetitions.

The difference engine was limited in its function. It produced its results only after particular numbers were "dialed in" by the operator. To do a different calculation, a new set of numbers had to be entered into the machine by hand. With Babbage's new machine, which he called an analytical engine, a series of cards (similar to those used by the weaving loom invented by Joseph Marie Jacquard) would contain instructions that would control the machine for each task. Some of the cards would determine what operations (addition, subtraction, multiplication, division, and so on) were to be performed, and in what order. Other cards would represent variables, or changeable quantities. This combination of instructions (or program code) and variables (representing each set of data, or numbers to be worked with) meant that the analytical engine was much more than a calculator. It was a general-purpose computer. Once properly programmed, it could work with any set of data cards.

As Babbage developed the design of the analytical engine further, he included other features found in today's computers. The analytical engine was to have a "mill," whose gears would calculate results. The mill corresponds to today's computer processor chips. Temporary results and the contents of variables would be kept in a large group of gears called the "store." This served the same purpose as memory chips in modern computers.

Babbage believed that the analytical engine would be even more mechanically complicated than the difference engine. Developing an analytical engine would be a very difficult and expensive task. Therefore Babbage needed to publicize his ideas and convince people to support his project. He went to Italy in 1840, hoping to interest Italian scientists in the machine. He was able to get an article written about his ideas.

When Babbage looked for someone to translate the Italian article into English so that it could be published in Britain as well, he found a

The whole of the developments and operations of analysis are now capable of being executed by machinery. . . . As soon as an Analytical Engine exits, it will necessarily guide the future course of science.

—Charles Babbage

Ada Lovelace was a pioneer woman mathematician—and perhaps the world's first computer programmer. (Science & Society Picture Library)

remarkable person for the job. In 1833, he had met a talented young woman named Ada Lovelace. Ada, born Ada Augusta Byron on December 10, 1815, was the daughter of the famous English poet Lord Byron. Byron, like many of the Romantic poets of the early 1800s, was a free-spirited, unconventional person. He was also a playboy and unfaithful to his wife. A year after Ada's birth, her father left, never to return.

Ada was raised by her mother, Annabella Milbanke Byron. Lady Byron was a remarkable woman with many intellectual interests in a time when few women were educated. Because of her love of mathematics, she was given the nickname "The Princess of Parallelograms." When young Ada also began to show a talent for mathematics, her mother encouraged her.

Lady Byron was much less encouraging in other ways. She was determined that Ada would be a proper young woman without any of her father's wildness. During lessons in arithmetic, grammar, spelling, and reading, Ada (like most five-year-old children) sometimes became restless. When this happened, Lady Byron made Ada lie perfectly still on a board. If she so much as moved her fingers, her hands were tied up in black bags. Under this intense discipline, Ada's feelings for her mother became a mixture of awe, fear, and a desire to please.

Like young Charles Babbage, Ada had serious health problems. She usually had a "nervous stomach" and sometimes had severe headaches. After an attack of measles, her legs were paralyzed for months. The only medical treatments available at the time, such as bleeding and bed rest, probably made Ada's condition worse.

Since there were no schools for women in the England of the early 1800s, Ada was taught by tutors hired by her mother. When she was about 19, Ada fell in love with a young tutor, and they briefly ran off together. Ada's mother hushed the matter up to avoid a scandal that might prevent Ada's future marriage. But Ada had shown that she could rebel against her mother's wishes, and Lady Byron redoubled her efforts to control her daughter's life.

Lady Byron introduced Ada to a respectable marriage prospect, Lord William King, who later became Lord Lovelace. Many marriages in aristocratic families were arranged for social and political reasons, but Ada and William shared a genuine love and married on July 8, 1835.

While marriage (and soon, a child) pleased Lovelace, they could not satisfy her restless need for mental exercise. Like her mother, she turned to mathematics. Mary Somerville, who had already become one of the first acknowledged woman mathematicians and scientists in England, encouraged Lovelace to apply herself to mathematics and served as her tutor as her studies grew more advanced.

Lovelace's biographers disagree about how good a mathematician she actually became. Augustus de Morgan, a noted logician who became her other important tutor, later wrote to her mother, "The power of thinking on these matters that Lady L. has always shown from the beginning of my correspondence with her, has been something so utterly out of the common way for any beginner, man or woman." Lovelace's mathematical ability, however, seemed to lie mainly in her intuitive grasp of the significance of mathematical concepts and their possible use. The questions she asked her tutors showed that she had trouble with the mechanics of mathematics. For example, she had difficulty learning how to solve mathematical equations by substituting or simplifying expressions—a skill needed even in basic algebra or trigonometry.

Perhaps it is most fair to say that Lovelace was not so much an accomplished mathematician as a first-rate thinker and writer *about* mathematics. These were just the talents Charles Babbage needed in someone who would work with him to popularize the concept of the analytical engine.

Working closely with Babbage, Lovelace translated the Italian article into "Sketch of the Analytical Engine Invented by Charles Babbage, Esq." When it was published, the title

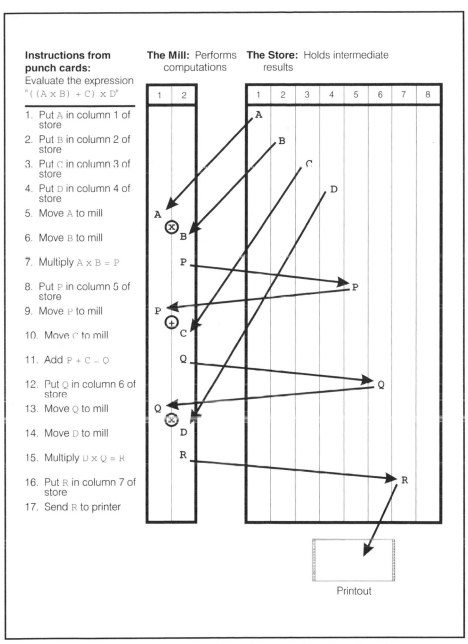

Instructions from punch cards:
Evaluate the expression
"((A x B) + C) x D"

1. Put A in column 1 of store
2. Put B in column 2 of store
3. Put C in column 3 of store
4. Put D in column 4 of store
5. Move A to mill
6. Move B to mill
7. Multiply A x B = P
8. Put P in column 5 of store
9. Move P to mill
10. Move C to mill
11. Add P + C = Q
12. Put Q in column 6 of store
13. Move Q to mill
14. Move D to mill
15. Multiply D x Q = R
16. Put R in column 7 of store
17. Send R to printer

The Mill: Performs computations

The Store: Holds intermediate results

Printout

A program for the difference engine. Numbers are first placed in the store, and then brought into the mill for calculations. Results of calculations can be saved in the store for future use.

(Courtesy of Katherine Macfarlane)

page said that it was "translated and with notes by A. A. L." The intials A. A. L. stood for Ada Augusta Lovelace, but the customs of the time did not allow a woman to use her full name in a book. Lovelace's "notes" really amounted to a separate paper that explored the possible application of the Analytical Engine to a variety of tasks, including even the automatic generation of music. She also added to the "diagrams" that showed the steps that would be used to instruct the analytical engine to solve particular problems. (Today we would call these "diagrams" computer programs.)

Babbage and Lovelace had begun to quarrel, however. Lovelace felt restrained by the limited role that she could play in the development of the analytical engine. She began to think of herself as "the High Priestess of Babbage's Engine," and her mind soared beyond the practical questions of computer design to ideas of uniting fields as diverse as science, mathematics, and poetry. Some modern doctors feel that Lovelace suffered from a manic-depressive condition. This meant that her moods could swing wildly. One day she would be bursting with energy and making ambitious plans. The next day, she would feel sad, depressed, and listless.

When Babbage scolded Lovelace for being too fanciful in her thinking, she began to correspond with other scientists, including Michael Fara-

> I never am really satisfied that I understand anything; because, understand it well as I may, my comprehension can only be an infinitesimal [tiny] fraction of all I want to understand about the many connections and relations which occur to me, how the matter in question was first thought of or arrived at, etc., etc.
>
> —Ada Lovelace

In 1991, a working model of Babbage's difference engine was built by researchers in the Science Museum, London. (Science & Society Picture Library)

day, who was revolutionizing science's understanding of electromagnetism. For a while, she even began to visit laboratories and help with electrical experiments. Unfortunately, she also experimented with gambling. To the horror of her husband and mother, she ran up major debts while betting on horse races.

In June 1851, Lovelace's doctor found that she had cancer of the uterus. Doctors could do nothing to treat this condition. Ada Lovelace spent the last few years of her life in great pain sometimes dulled by doses of morphine. She died on November 27, 1852, at the age of only 36.

Charles Babbage, on the other hand, lived to be almost 80 years old. He never succeeded in raising the funds to build his analytical engine. The idea of an automatic computer faded from public view. Babbage did important work, however, in the development and use of statistics for economic and social research. He died on October 18, 1871.

Modern computer scientists have celebrated the memory of Charles Babbage and Ada Lovelace. In 1991, a hundred years after Babbage's death, researchers at the Science Museum in London built a complete, fully functional Babbage difference engine. They were careful to use only parts that Babbage could have built. Their work suggests that given more cooperation and funds, his "number loom" might have become a reality.

In the late 1970s, the United States government designed a new computer language to be used for its data processing needs. The language was named Ada, in honor of Ada Lovelace.

Chronology

December 26, 1791	Charles Babbage born
1810	enters Trinity College, Cambridge
1815	elected to British Royal Society
December 10, 1815	Ada Augusta Byron born
1820–1822	Babbage builds model of difference engine
1832–1834	Babbage stops building Difference Engine Number One, begins to develop analytical engine
1833	Ada Byron meets Charles Babbage
July 8, 1835	Byron marries Lord William King (later Lord Lovelace)
1840	Ada begins intensive study of mathematics with Augustus De Morgan

da publishes translation of article on the
nalytical Engine, with extensive notes

da Lovelace dies

harles Babbage dies

.S. government names new program-
ing language Ada

odel of Babbage difference engine built

ers of Computing. London: Frederick
>rt, readable chapter introducing Bab-

harles Babbage: Father of the Com-
ell Collier Press, 1970. Detailed biog-
;e written for young adults.

mbers: Lives of Women Mathemati-
tivities. San Carlos, California: Wide
1993. Another good source for learn-
maticians. Chapter on Ada Lovelace
;ramming activity.

nd a Legacy. Cambridge, Mass.: MIT
Ada Lovelace's life that looks at her
, ways of thinking, and health.

ring Charles Babbage's Mechanical
ierican, February 1993. Explains the
lifference engine and describes how
lete working model from Babbage's

mathemati-
Library)

George Boole devised the theory of sets. He also developed rules of cal *logic used in today's computer circuits.* (Science & Society Pictur

George Boole

(1815–1864)

A student sits down at a library computer terminal. She is preparing to write a report on global warming for her science class. She chooses "search for article titles" from the menu, and then types "global warming."

The computer swiftly scans its indexes. It finds all the titles that include the word *global* and all the titles that contain the word *warming*. The computer then compares the two sets of titles and extracts from them the titles that have *both* words. It displays these titles on the terminal.

Our student probably doesn't know it, but the library computer is using rules of logic invented by George Boole, an English mathematician, almost a century before practical computers existed.

George Boole was born on November 2, 1815, in Lincoln, England, though his family soon moved to London. His father, John Boole, was a former shoemaker and now a shop owner. John Boole's heart wasn't really in his trade, however. His first love was science. He loved to talk with people of learning about the discoveries of the day. John performed his own experiments and built scientific instruments. For example, he built a large telescope and then put a sign in his shop window that said, "Anyone who wishes to observe the works of God in a spirit of reverence is invited to come and look through my telescope."

George's schooling began when he was only a year and a half old. His teachers found him very bright and inquisitive. At about kindergarten age, he disappeared from home one day. After an anxious search he was found in downtown London, surrounded by a crowd of amazed people, spelling out hard words and being rewarded with a shower of coins.

At age seven George went to primary school. A fellow student recalled, "He was not of my class, or indeed of any class; for we had no boy in the school equal to him and perhaps the master was not, though he professed to teach him."

George's father also played an important part in his education, introducing him to English literature, elementary mathematics, and geometry. They built cameras, telescopes, and microscopes together. Although George Boole would become famous as a pure, abstract mathematician, he would always keep a strong interest in applied science—a combination of interests shared by Charles Babbage.

Despite his talents, the Boole family couldn't afford to provide George with a university education. Instead, George went to a commercial or vocational school, where he continued his literary studies and mastered advanced algebra. He then had to decide on a career. For an educated and talented young man of the lower middle class, there seemed to be only two real possibilities: the clergy and teaching.

Boole had strong religious feelings from an early age. He shared his father's belief that science, by uncovering the mysteries of God's creation, brought people closer to the divine. But he wasn't comfortable with the strict beliefs of the Church of England, being closer to the liberal spirit of the Unitarian faith. More important, because his father's shop had failed, George Boole, even though he was only 16 years old, became responsible for supporting his family.

Teaching paid a little better than being a minister, so Boole decided to become a teacher.

Boole first worked as a teaching assistant at a Methodist school run by a Mr. Heigham. He was dismissed from this job because of religious disagreements and a tendency to get absorbed in his own studies. (It was reported that Boole did mathematics problems on Sundays, even while sitting in chapel.) Later positions at Doncaster and Liverpool also brought Boole problems, but he persevered. He later did well in a position at the village of Waddington.

Boole's interest in mathematics grew considerably during this time. Starting at age 16, he had begun to buy mathematics textbooks such as the *Differential and Integral Calculus* of Lacroix, a French mathematician. Without the benefit of college training, he didn't know which books were best. He learned to rely instead on his own understanding, which helped prepare him for the strikingly original work he would do later.

As his parents grew older and their health declined, Boole became more concerned about his family's future. His salary as an assistant teacher wasn't nearly enough to provide for their needs. In 1834, therefore, at the age of 19, he took a bold gamble: He started his own school. His philosophy of education was rather modern. He believed in a balanced curriculum that included languages, literature, and science. He insisted that mathematics students needed to apply the abstract rules they were learning to real physical objects.

Boole's school was quite successful. He also became involved with the Mechanic's Institute, an organization dedicated to improving the education of the working class. Overcoming a certain shyness about speaking in public, he began to give lectures. In one lecture, he showed how Isaac Newton's calculus had revealed itself to be a powerful tool for understanding the physical world.

Since the time of Newton two centuries earlier, British mathematics had fallen behind that of other European nations. Following Newton's lead, mathematicians in Britain remained closely tied to diagrams of motions of physical objects such as planets. European mathematics, following Gottfried Leibniz's version of calculus, dealt with mathematical symbols and operations in a more abstract and flexible way. Along with Charles Babbage and William Herschel, Boole formed the Analytical Society, which tried to reform British mathematics along European lines.

In his effort to find a new direction for mathematics, Boole read and absorbed the work of French mathematicians, notably Joseph-Louis Lagrange, who had created an abstract set of mathematical descriptions of the motions and interactions of physical bodies. At the age of 23, Boole submitted his first scientific paper, which offered improvements to Lagrange's methods.

Boole's paper focused not on the mathematical description of the physical world but on the nature of the mathematical operations and symbols themselves. These symbols have laws of their own: For example, the plus symbol, or +, follows a law called *commutation*. Commutation means that an addition gives the same result regardless of the order in which you add the numbers: 2 + 4 is the same as 4 + 2. (The minus symbol does not have this property: 5 − 2 does not equal 2 − 5.) Boole's paper showed the beginning of his interest in the connection between mathematical symbols and the process of human thought.

In 1844, Boole submitted a paper with the title "On a General Method in Analysis" to the Royal Society, Britain's most prestigious scientific organization. In this paper, Boole continued his systematic look at the use of mathematical symbols. Boole began to write papers regularly.

Apparently, most of the members of the Council of the Royal Society at first rejected Boole's paper without even reading it. Perhaps they may have been prejudiced by Boole's relatively low social class or his lack of a university degree.

Exactly what happened next is unclear, but it seems that a member of the Society objected to the way Boole was being treated and demanded that the paper receive a fair hearing. Eventually, the paper was not only accepted for publication in the *Transactions* of the Royal Society, but was awarded a special prize—the first gold medal ever awarded by the society for mathematics.

As Boole became more involved with current developments in mathematics, he began to feel isolated. As a mere provincial schoolteacher, he had no peers with whom he could regularly discuss academic matters. He also felt that his lack of a university education handicapped him professionally, despite the growing reputation that his papers had begun to bring him. He visited Cambridge and considered studying for a degree there, but he decided he couldn't afford to do so.

In 1846 a group of institutions called Queen's Colleges were being founded in Ireland, and Boole decided to apply for a professorship in mathematics in this new college system. He had received excellent letters of recommendation that more than made up for his lack of a university degree, but the selection process was excruciatingly slow. Finally, in 1849, he received an appointment as professor of mathematics at Queen's College, Cork. Boole was successful at this post, which he held for the rest of his working life.

Boole was now on the threshold of his great work on logic. In a postscript to his 1844 Royal Society paper, he had noted that "any great advance in the higher analysis must be sought for by an increased atten-

[This work] is designed, in the first place, to investigate the fundamental laws of those operations of the mind by which reasoning is performed.

—George Boole

tion to the laws of the combinations of symbols." In 1847 he began to apply his study of symbols to the laws of logic. (Logic is the study of the relationships between statements and of the methods for proving statements to be true.) Boole's interest in logic may have sprung from his lifelong interest in language and grammar, which have their own logical structure. Boole created a new kind of algebra whose symbols could represent and manipulate logical statements.

A key idea of Boole's symbolic logic is the concept of a *set*. A set is a group of objects that share a certain characteristic. For example, the set of animals consists of dogs, cats, birds, fish, and many other creatures. All objects in this set share the characteristics of life and movement.

Within the set of animals there are many "subsets," such as the set of dogs. Boole showed that many of the laws that applied to ordinary algebra could also be applied to sets. For example, if x is the subset of dogs and 1 is the "universe" or complete set of animals, the set of all animals that are *not* dogs can be expressed as $1 - x$. If you add dogs and "nondogs" together, you get $x + (1 - x)$, which simply works out to 1. In other words, the *union* or combination of the set of dogs and the set of nondogs is the set of all animals.

Similarly, Boole showed that sets had a commutative relationship like that of ordinary numbers. For example, "dogs + nondogs" is exactly the same thing as "nondogs + dogs." Mathematically, this is expressed as $1 + (1 - x) = (1 - x) + 1$.

The *intersection* of two sets is the set of elements or items that are found in both sets. When the student asked for articles on global warming, the library computer found the intersection of the set of titles containing the word *global* and the set of titles containing the word *warming*. Intersections are also commutative: Whether the computer started with the "global" titles or the "warming" ones, the result of the search would be the same.

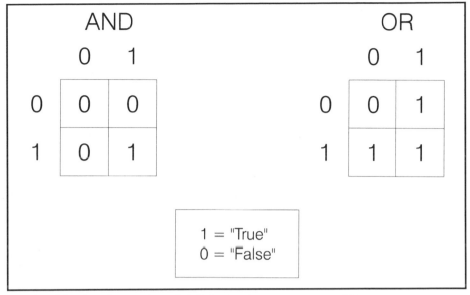

Truth tables for the AND and OR logic. 1 means true, and 0 means false. AND is true if both statements are true. OR is true if either statement is true. Read down and across to see the result. (Courtesy of Katherine Macfarlane)

Boole used special symbols, or operators, to stand for *and* and *or*. These symbols could be used to express logical propositions, or statements about whether something was true or false or whether an object belonged to a particular set. He also created "truth tables" that summarized what happened when two statements were combined.

Boole carried on this system to a much more complex level. He first described it in a pamphlet, *The Mathematical Analysis of Logic*, in 1847, where his new algebra of logic won an enthusiastic response from Augustus De Morgan, a noted logician. In 1854 Boole published his most important work, *An Investigation into the Laws of Thought, on Which Are Founded the Mathematical Theories of Logic and Probabilities*. He would do other important work later on differential equations and calculus, but this work on logic is Boole's most enduring achievement.

Boole's reference to "Laws of Thought" indicated a broader interest than just mathematics: Boole believed that just as Newton's calculus could uncover the laws that governed physical motion, his logical algebra could begin to uncover truths about psychology.

Meanwhile, Boole had met a young woman named Mary Everest, the niece of one of his colleagues at Cork. Boole was sociable and friendly, but for some years he had lacked the money to support a family. The friendship that grew between George and Mary therefore was tentative, with Boole acting mostly as the young woman's tutor and advisor. But in 1855, after Mary's father died, her need for support and the growing love between her and Boole quickly led to marriage. It was a happy one and the Booles had five children, all daughters.

Both George and Mary Boole had often suffered from ill health. In late 1864, Boole made the mistake of walking three miles through the cold rain. He developed a form of pneumonia and died on December 8. He was only 49 years old. It is sad to contemplate the further work he might have done if he had lived longer.

Today switching circuits and computer logic are laid out using the rules Boole created. The 1 and 0 of

Mary Boole, writing in 1884, looked toward the computerized future:

"Within the last generation we have gained a 'Calculating Engine,' a 'Calculus of Logic' (with many and widespread applications), a 'Logical Abacus'; and we are fast discovering means of making the generation of the most complicated and beautiful curves as mechanical a process as Logic has become. Of what are these inventions a sign?"

Boolean logic are also the "on" and "off" bits that encode the text and other data that streak along the "information highway."

Chronology

November 2, 1815	George Boole born in Lincoln, England
1831	begins career as a schoolteacher
1834	opens his own school in Lincoln
1839	begins to write papers on mathematics
1844	paper "On a General Method in Analysis" published by Royal Society and awarded a gold medal
1847	pamphlet *Mathematical Analysis of Logic* introduces Boolean algebra
1849	Boole appointed to professorship at Queen's College, Cork
1854	publishes *An Investigation into the Laws of Thought*, his major work on logic
1855	marries Mary Everest
December 8, 1864	George Boole dies

Further Reading

Kramer, Edna E. *The Nature and Growth of Modern Mathematics*. Princeton, New Jersey: Princeton University Press, 1981. Chapter 6 discusses the development of mathematical logic by Boole, De Morgan, and others.

MacHale, Desmond. *George Boole: His Life and Work*. Dublin: Boole Press, 1985. A quite readable biography of Boole with light treatment of the mathematics.

Georg Cantor extended the idea of sets to compare infinite series of numbers. He showed that there was more than one kind of "infinity."

Georg Cantor

(1845–1918)

Zeno, an ancient Greek thinker, came up with a puzzle that stumped everyone who heard it. He asked them to imagine a race between Achilles, a great hero and athlete, and a tortoise. Achilles was a much faster runner than the tortoise was. While Achilles covered a distance of 100 yards, the tortoise could barely crawl a single yard. Suppose the tortoise were given a hundred-yard head start. When would Achilles overtake the tortoise? The surprising answer, according to Zeno, was "never."

Imagine: The starting gun goes off, and Achilles races for 100 yards, reaching the place where the tortoise had started. Meanwhile, the tortoise moves ahead one yard. Suppose, Zeno said, that Achilles quickly covers that remaining yard. While Achilles is doing that, however, the tortoise has moved a little bit farther forward. Achilles covers that distance in a flash—but the meanwhile, the tortoise has moved ahead a tiny distance. If you look at the race as a series of moves by Achilles and the tortoise, Achilles never quite catches up.

In real life, of course, Achilles quickly runs past the tortoise. But Zeno's listeners couldn't show how his reasoning was wrong. It would be about 2,400 years until a mathematician named Georg Cantor would be able to solve the puzzle. To do so, he would have to change the way people thought about the idea of infinity.

Georg Cantor was born on March 3, 1845, in St. Petersburg, Russia. His father, Georg Woldemar Cantor, was a merchant who had been born in Copenhagen, Denmark. Although he was of Jewish ancestry, he had converted to the Lutheran faith. Georg's mother, Maria Anna Bolm, came from a family that had great artistic and musical talent. The combination of religious devotion and a creative imagination would help drive Georg toward a breakthrough in mathematics.

From elementary school through high school Georg showed talent in both music and drawing. He became interested in the study of theology, philosophy, and literature. Mathematics seemed to attract the young man most strongly, however.

When Georg was ready for college, he and his father disagreed about choosing a career. Georg wanted to study pure, or theoretical, mathematics. His father, however, had been a very successful businessperson. He saw the growing demand for trained engineers who could put scientific knowledge to practical use. He urged his son to study engineering. Georg resisted this advice, and his father eventually backed down and let him study mathematics.

In 1862, Cantor began his higher education at the Polytechnikum in Zurich, Switzerland. Since childhood, he had sometimes had periods of mental depression, and this condition now returned. (Some modern psychologists believe that Georg Cantor, like Ada Lovelace, suffered from a manic-depressive condition.) The death of Cantor's father from tuberculosis in 1863 also saddened him. He had gone to the Polytechnikum because its courses in applied, or practical, mathematics pleased his engineering-minded father. Now, however, he was free to go to the university at Berlin, Germany. This school had the best professors in pure mathematics. It also had great prestige, and its graduates had the best chance to find employment as university professors.

In 1867, Cantor received his doctor's degree from Berlin, magna cum laude (with high honors). In 1869, he went to work at the Martin Luther University in Halle, Germany. In 1874, he married Valle Guttman. At Halle, Cantor did good research in analysis (advanced calculus). One of the things he studied was series of numbers based on the ratios called sines (pronounced like *signs*) and cosines that are found in basic trigonometry (the study of the relationships of angles and sides of triangles). Some of these series involved the mysterious quantity called "infinity."

Infinity is a difficult concept. Many people think that infinity is simply a gigantic number that would take forever to count up to. But infinity is not really a number. An ordinary number, however large, cannot be infinity, because another number (such as one) can always be added to it to make a still larger number.

Even mathematicians were uncomfortable with the idea of infinity. Most mathematicians were content to use infinity simply as a boundary or limit for a series of numbers. For example, in the series $^1/_{.1}$ (one divided by one-tenth), $^1/_{.01}$ (one divided by one-hundredth), $^1/_{.001}$, $^1/_{.0001}$, and so on, the quantities grow larger and larger as the divisor grows smaller and smaller. The series can be said to "approach a limit of infinity." But what *was* infinity? Could you show that something amounted to infinity, without actually counting it? Could there be more than one kind of infinity? Between 1874 and the end of the century, Cantor wrote a series of papers that tried to answer these questions.

Cantor's new approach to infinity was based on the idea of sets. A set is collection of objects—in mathematics, a set is usually a collection of numbers. For example, the set of positive natural numbers (also called integers, or counting numbers) begins 1, 2, 3, . . . Intuitively, it is easy to see that this is an infinite set, since it can never be counted to the end. But what about other sets of numbers such as the even numbers or rational numbers (numbers that are made up of ratios, or fractions)? Are these also infinite sets? If they are, are they the "same kind" of infinite set as the positive integers?

Clearly it is not possible to count up the members in these sets to see if they are "equally infinite." Instead, Cantor hit on the idea of using a process of *matching* to compare sets. For example, consider the set of even numbers. This set is a subset of the set of whole numbers (that is, the set of all even numbers is contained in the set of all whole numbers. The set of all whole numbers also contains the odd numbers, of course.)

Cantor pointed out that each whole number (1, 2, 3, . . .) could be matched with an even number (2, 4, 6, . . .) There is exactly one even number for each whole number, with nothing left over. This sort of relationship is called a one-to-one correspondence. Intuitively, you might suppose that the set of even numbers is exactly half the size of the set of whole numbers, since half of all numbers are even, and the other half, odd. But since the set of whole numbers can be matched with its subset (even numbers) on a one-to-one basis with nothing ever being left over, Cantor said that the sets are actually both equal—equally infinite! In general, Cantor said that any set that can be matched one to one with the positive whole numbers is a *countably infinite* set.

What about rational numbers? Rational numbers are expressed as fractions, such as $1/2$ or $2/3$ (whole numbers are also rational numbers: for example $2/1$ is 2, $3/1$ is 3, and so on). Is the set of rational numbers also countably infinite? To prove that this is so, the set of rational numbers would

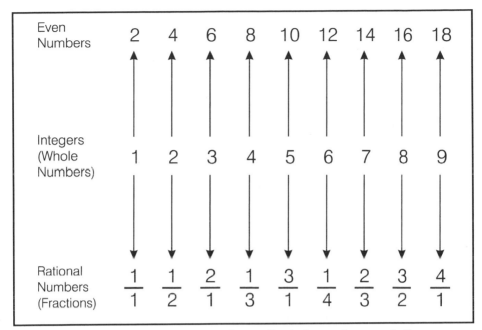

A number line showing the even numbers, all whole numbers, and all rational numbers, or fractions. Since all three sets can be matched one for one, Cantor called them "countably infinite." (Courtesy of Katherine Macfarlane)

have to be put into a one-to-one correspondence with the set of positive whole numbers. Cantor hit on a clever way of doing this. First, he said, take all the fractions whose numerator (the number on top) and denominator (the number on the bottom) add up to 2. There's only one, $^1/_1$, so match that to the whole number 1. Next, look at the fractions whose numerators add up to 3. There are two of these: $^1/_2$ and $^2/_1$. Match 2 and 3 to them. There are three fractions whose numerators add up to 4: $^1/_3$, $^2/_2$, and $^3/_1$. Match 4 to $^1/_3$, drop $^2/_2$ (because it's not in lowest terms), and match 5 to $^3/_1$. This process can be continued forever, with each fraction having a whole number matched to it. Cantor thus showed that the rational numbers were countably infinite.

Cantor's idea of infinity also explained what Zeno was really doing in his puzzle. Zeno was taking each position reached by the tortoise and "matching" to it the time it took Achilles to catch up to that position. Since the tortoise, no matter how slow, can reach an infinite number of new positions, each new position of the tortoise can always be matched to a movement by Achilles that just catches up to it—each movement taking a smaller and smaller amount of time. Zeno was setting up a one-to-one correpondence between the times taken by Achilles and the successive positions of the tortoise. According to Cantor, this one-to-one correspondence means that the two series are "equally infinite" and can be extended indefinitely. But in reality, of course, if you use fixed intervals of time (such as one second), you will soon come to a second in which Achilles overtakes the tortoise.

Not all infinities are countable, however. Cantor also considered the real numbers. The set of real numbers includes whole numbers and fractions, but it also includes irrational numbers (numbers that cannot be expressed as a ratio: for example, the square root of two). Suppose, Cantor said, one made a list of all the possible real numbers in decimal form (such as 1.319148, 1.527843, and so on, but with an infinite number of decimal places). Cantor showed that no matter how long you made your list, you could always change the decimal places in a way that made a new number that *wasn't* on the list. This meant that the set of real numbers was uncountably infinite.

Cantor then said that uncountably infinite sets like that of the real numbers were "more" infinite than sets such as the whole numbers or rational numbers. To show the different degrees or kinds of infinity, Cantor used the Hebrew letter aleph ($\aleph$) with a subscript showing the degree of infiniteness, which he called *cardinality*. Thus Cantor assigned the value $\aleph_0$ (pronounced aleph-zero) to the whole numbers and rational numbers and the value $\aleph_1$ (aleph-one) to the real numbers. Cantor later showed that the set of all subsets of real numbers (that is, the number of ways the real numbers can be grouped into smaller sets) had a still higher cardinality, $\aleph_2$. In fact, Cantor showed that there was an infinite number of "aleph numbers"—an infinity of infinities!

Many mathematicians did not accept Cantor's new ideas about infinity. In part, their opposition was probably due to the strangeness of this new way of thinking. Earlier in the 19th century, the great mathematician Carl Friedrich Gauss had said " . . . I protest above all against the use of an infinite quantity as a *completed* one, which in mathematics is never allowed. The Infinite is only a manner of speaking." Cantor, on the other hand, had used set theory and matching to "complete" and categorize the kinds of infinity.

But Cantor himself tended to make it hard for his colleagues to accept his ideas. Because of his strong religious beliefs, he often spoke of infinity in mystical terms that were uncomfortable to scientists. Also, his mental problems often led him to lash out violently against critics.

The Martin Luther University at Halle, where Cantor had worked for many years, was considered by many a second class institution. Cantor badly wanted a position at the University at Berlin, and he increasingly felt that one of his harshest critics, Leopold Kronecker, was blocking his advancement. The dispute grew

I entertain no doubts as to the truths of the transfinities, which I recognized with God's help and which, in their diversity, I have studied for more than twenty years; every year, and almost every day brings me further in this science.

—Georg Cantor

more bitter. In 1884, Cantor suffered the first of what would be a series of nervous breakdowns. Until his death in 1918, Cantor would be in and out of the hospital for treatment of his condition.

Despite his problems, Cantor continued to believe that his work was correct and would survive. Discussing his work on infinity, he asserted that "this view, which I consider to be the sole correct one, is held by only a few. While possibly I am the very first in history to take this position so explicitly, with all of its logical consequences, I know for sure that I won't be the last."

Cantor's faith in his work proved to be correct. In the 20th century, researchers in set theory and infinite series filled in the gaps in Cantor's theories.

Chronology

March 3, 1845	Georg Cantor born in St. Petersburg, Russia
1862	begins college at the Polytechnikum in Zurich, Switzerland
1863	Cantor's father dies; Cantor moves to the University in Berlin, Germany
1867–1869	Cantor receives his doctorate and begins to work at the Martin Luther University, Halle, Germany
1874	begins to write papers about infinite sets of numbers; marries Valle Guttmann
1884	suffers first nervous breakdown
January 6, 1918	Cantor dies

Further Reading

Ashurst, F. Gareth. *Founders of Modern Mathematics*. London: Frederick Muller, 1982. Chapter 6 briefly summarizes Cantor's life and work.

Dunham, William. *Journey through Genius: The Great Theorems of Mathematics*. New York: John Wiley & Sons, 1990. A good introduction to the milestones of mathematical achievement, suitable for high school students. Chapters 11 and 12 deal with Cantor's work.

Paulos, John Allen. *Beyond Numeracy: Ruminations of a Numbers Man*. New York: Vintage Books, 1991. Makes mathematics concepts understandable for readers from junior high school up. "Infinite Sets" summarizes Cantor's basic ideas.

Sofia Kovalevskaia. This Russian-born mathematician became the first woman to hold a full university professorship in modern Europe. She won the Bordin Prize for her solution to the problem of Saturn's rings. (© Photographer, Science Source/Photo Researchers)

Sofia Kovalevskaia

(1850–1891)

From time to time the French Academy of Science offered an award called the Bordin Prize for the best solution to a specified mathematical problem. In 1888, the prize was to be awarded for the best paper dealing with the motion of a solid body around a fixed point—a topic of great interest to astronomers and physicists who were studying the behavior of planets, moons, and the mysterious rings of Saturn.

The academy received fifteen papers for this competition. To make sure that the judges would not be swayed by anyone's reputation, the author's names were left out of the papers and a motto or phrase was used for identification.

The judges felt that one paper stood out from the rest. The paper considered how the rings of Saturn were able to stay in a stable orbit around the planet. According to the judges, "The author's method of solving the problem . . . allows him to give a complete solution in the most precise and elegant form."

When the winning entry was announced, the sealed envelope containing the name of the paper's author was opened. It had turned out that the judges of the French Academy had used the wrong pronoun in describing this particular author's work. To the great astonishment of the scientific community, the prize-winning mathemati-

cian was not a "him." She was a woman named Sofia
Kovalevskaia (Kov-a-lev-sky-ah).

Sofia Corvin-Krukovskaia (Kru-kov-sky-ah) was born in
Moscow in 1850. (Some sources give her first name as
Sonya.) Her father was a general in the army of the Russian
czar. As in most noble families in Europe, Sofia did not see
much of her parents as she was growing up. Her upbringing
was handled by an English governess who was also her only
teacher until she was 12 years old. Like Ada Lovelace, Sofia
was raised with strict discipline that was intended to make
her a "proper young lady."

Sofia had a strong will of her own, however, as well as a
lively imagination. When she was about six years old, Sofia's
father retired from the army. The family moved to a remote
estate in the countryside at Palinbo, near the border between
Russia and Lithuania. The isolation of this place meant that
Sofia often had to find her own sources of amusement.

The large house was decorated with fancy imported wall-
paper, but the wallpaper had run out before the rooms did.
The family had to resort to a temporary wall covering, as
Sofia noted in recalling her childhood.

> By a happy coincidence the paper used for this first
> covering consisted of sheets of Ostrogradsky's litho-
> graphed lectures on the differential and the integral
> calculus, bought by my father in his youth. These sheets,
> spotted over with strange incomprehensible formulae,
> soon attracted my attention. I remember how . . . I
> passed whole hours before that mysterious wall, trying
> to decipher even a single phrase, and to discover the
> order in which the sheets ought to follow each other.

An interest in mathematics seemed to run in the Kru-
kovsky family: Sofia's grandfather had been a mathematician

and head topographer (mapper of land forms) for the army. Her great-grandfather had been a mathematician and astronomer. But Sophia's most important early exposure to science came from long conversations about mathematics and philosophy with her uncle Piotr, who told her about such ideas as "squaring the circle" and the paths of curved lines called asymptotes that almost, but not quite, touched other lines as they reached toward infinity.

When Sofia was 12, her governess left. Sofia was determined to continue her studies on her own. She became interested in physics, so she borrowed a book from a neighbor who was a physicist. The physics book had unfamiliar formulas in it. The formulas were related to trigonometry (the study of the relationships of angles and sides of triangles). Sofia had no book on trigonometry, but she painstakingly worked out the formulas from scratch. Much to the surprise of the neighbor, Sofia "had created that whole branch of science—trigonometry—a second time." He was so impressed with what the young woman had done that he talked her father into letting her study with a tutor in the nearest city, St. Petersburg.

After a couple years of study in St. Petersburg, Sofia seemed to reach a dead end. By then she had chosen mathematics for a career, but no Russian university accepted women as students. Some universities in other countries did accept women students, but there was another problem. Sofia's father opposed her career plans. Russian women could not travel freely. A woman was listed on her father's passport until she married, at which time she became her husband's responsibility.

Meanwhile, Sofia's older sister Aniuta had shown her own streak of independence. She had written a story that was published in a magazine edited by Fyodor Dostoevsky, a famous Russian novelist. Dostoevsky introduced both Ani-

I understand your surprise at my being able to busy myself simultaneously with literature and mathematics. Many who have never had an opportunity of knowing any more about mathematics confound [confuse] it with arithmetic, and consider it to be an arid science. In reality, however, it is a science which requires a great amount of imagination, and one of the leading mathematicians of our century states the case quite correctly when he says that it is impossible to be a mathematician without being a poet in soul.

—Sofia Kovalevskaia

uta and Sofia to friends who shared the radical political ideas that were starting to sweep through Russia.

The Russian nobility that Sofia's father belonged to was very conservative. In a way Russia had only just left the Middle Ages, having abolished serfdom only a few years earlier. But a new philosophy called nihilism was becoming popular with Russian artists, writers, and students. Somewhat like the hippies of the 1960s, the nihilists of the 1860s questioned all authority. They advocated freedom of expression, socialism, and equality for women. Sofia and Aniuta eagerly embraced these new ideas. Many young women who followed nihilist ideas had found that they could break free of their parents' control by getting married "on paper" to a willing man. It was understood that in such marriages the couple would not live together as husband and wife, and the woman would be free to travel on her own. As a married woman, Sofia could travel abroad and continue her mathematical studies.

In 1868, Sofia met and married a man named Vladimir Kovalevsky. Vladimir, a geology student, was sympathetic to women's desire for freedom, and he was impressed by Sofia's mathematical and literary talents as well as by her beauty. They went together to the famous German university at Heidelberg. There, Sofia began her formal study of higher mathematics.

Kovalevskaia (the feminine form of *Kovalevsky*) made a strong impression on the students and faculty members she met at Heidelberg. After two years of study at Heidelberg, Kovalevskaia decided to go to Berlin. She hoped that she could study with Karl T. Weierstrass, who was widely considered to be Europe's leading expert in the kinds of mathematical functions that were closely related to mechanics, the study of moving bodies. (Kovalevskaia had always been interested in physics and astronomy, so it's not surprising that she became especially interested in those parts of mathematics that could be used to explain the phenomena of those sciences.)

When she arrived in 1870, however, Kovalevskaia learned that the Berlin University, like those in Russia, would not accept women. The fact that she had brought letters from former professors that were filled with glowing recommendations made no difference.

Kovalevskaia could not be stopped for long, however. She asked Weierstrass to give her private lessons. Weierstrass, perhaps trying to get rid of her, started by giving Kovalevskaia a set of problems that were normally done only by his most advanced students. Much to his astonishment, she quickly solved them—in some cases coming up with original and imaginative solutions. Weierstrass then agreed to take Kovalevskaia as a student. He even tried to get her admitted to his lectures, but the university administration remained rigid and unyielding and refused to change its rules forbidding women. Weierstrass helped compensate for this by giving Kovalevskaia copies of his lecture notes and unpublished papers.

After four years of study with Weierstrass, Kovalevskaia wrote her doctoral dissertation "On the Theory of Partial Differential Equations." A *differential equation* is a mathematical statement that describes how a change in one quantity, or variable, is related to a change in one or more other quantities. More specifically, a mathematical expression called a *derivative* can show the rate at which some quantity changes. This kind of equation is particularly useful for describing physical phenomena such as motion.

For example, if you get in a car and drive for one hour, the distance you travel will depend on the car's speed in miles per hour. The speed (or more technically, the velocity) can be said to be the *derivative* of the distance traveled—for a given period of time: the greater the distance, the greater the speed. A derivative can itself have a derivative: if you get in a parked car, start the engine, and step on the accelerator until the car is moving 50 miles an hour, the car's speed is steadily increasing throughout this time. This change is speed is called acceleration. The rate of acceleration is the derivative of the velocity, which in turn is the derivative of the distance traveled. Mathematicians say that acceleration is the "second derivative" of distance.

Differential equations can be used to solve a variety of problems in science. An astronomer can use them to study rotating planets or revolving moons. An economist can use them to study how fast the rate of inflation is increasing. Kovalevskaia's contribution to the theory of differential equations is that she showed how to determine how much information (data) was needed to solve a given type (or order) of partial differential equation.

Kovalevskaia wrote two more papers, each sufficient in itself to earn a doctoral degree. Despite her not having attended classes, the quality of her work and the recommendations of her teachers proved to be irresistible. She received her doctor's degree from the University of Göttingen in 1874.

Weierstrass tried to help Kovalevskaia get a teaching job. But despite her degree and her growing reputation, the answer was always the same: ". . . but she's a woman."

Finally, Kovalevskaia returned to Russia. Vladimir had been pursuing his own studies and had become a professor of paleontology (the study of ancient living things) in Moscow. The relationship between Sofia and Vladimir gradually began to change. The "marriage on paper" became a real love relationship. In 1878, Sofia and Vladimir had a daughter, Sofia. Kovalevskaia brought the same passion and intensity to her new role of wife and mother that she had brought to her mathematics and writing.

But Vladimir began to lose interest in science. He made bad business investments and lost most of his money. The marriage began to unravel. Sofia took her daughter and went back to Berlin. Weierstrass helped her return to mathematical work. She wrote a new mathematical paper on how light refracted, or bent, when passing through a crystal. Meanwhile, Vladimir grew more desperate. Then he killed himself. Sofia was shocked by the news and took months to recover from her feelings of guilt and depression. Finally, however, she resolved to continue her career in mathematics.

Despite Weierstrass's efforts, there were no jobs to be had for a woman mathematician in Germany. But another student of Weierstrass, Göstag Mittag-Leffler, had become a professor of mathematics at the new University of Stockholm, Sweden. The Swedes had a more liberal attitude toward opportunities for women than that found in most of Europe. Kovalevskaia and Mittag-Leffler had become friends. In 1883, he was able to get her a job as a lecturer. In 1889 she would become the first woman in modern Europe to become a full tenured (permanent) professor.

Göstag Mittag-Leffler's brother wrote a poem in memory of Sofia Kovalevskaia, calling her "the Muse of the Heavens":

While Saturn's rings still shine,
While mortals breathe,
The world will ever remember your name.

Kovalevskaia returned to her mathematical work. She decided to enter the competition for the Bordin Prize, one of the highest awards given in mathematics. Kovalevskaia's paper for the Bordin Prize contest dealt with the problem of how the rings of the planet Saturn managed to rotate around the planet. To solve this problem, she drew on the work of Weierstrass and of the French astronomer and mathematician Pierre Simon de Laplace. Kovalevskaia went beyond this earlier work and devised a more complete differential equation. This equation showed that Saturn's rings were not shaped like an ellipse, as astronomers had thought. Rather, a cross section through a ring formed a kind of "lopsided" egg shape.

Shortly after winning the Bordin Prize, Sofia met a man named Maxim Kovalevsky (a distant relation of her late husband Vladimir). They fell in love, but their relationship was a stormy one. In 1891, after spending a vacation in France with Maxim, Sofia boarded a train heading back to Sweden. Riding the drafty cars in the cold and rain, Sofia caught a cold and eventually came down with pneumonia. She died at the age of only 41. In 1951, just after the hundredth anniversary of her birth, the Soviet Union honored her with a postage stamp.

Kovalevskaia's prize-winning paper for the French Academy had used the motto "Say what you know, do what you must, come what may." It would be hard to find a better way to sum up the life and work of this remarkable pioneer woman mathematician.

Chronology

January 15, 1850	Sofia Corvin-Krukovskaia born in St. Petersburg, Russia
1868	Sofia and Vladimir Kovalevsky have marriage of convenience

1870	Sofia begins to study with Karl T. Weierstrass
1874	receives doctorate from Göttingen University; returns to live with Vladimir Kovalevsky
1878	has a daughter, Sofia
1880	leaves Vladimir Kovalevsky and returns to mathematical work
1883	gets temporary teaching post in Stockholm University
1888	wins Prix Bordin from French Academy for paper on spinning motion
1889	becomes first tenured woman professor in Europe
February 1891	Sofia Kovalevskaia dies

Further Reading

Abir-Am, Pnina G., and Dorinda Outram, eds. *Uneasy Careers and Intimate Lives: Women in Science, 1789–1979*. New Brunswick: Rutgers University Press, 1987. Chapter entitled "Career and Home Life in the 1880s: The Choices of Mathematician Sofia Kovalevskaia" discusses how she made decisions about her marriage, child, and career opportunities.

Kennedy, Don H. *Little Sparrow: A Portrait of Sophia Kovalevsky*. Athens, Ohio: Ohio University Press, 1983. Detailed biography of Kovalevskaia; not much detail on her mathematics.

Osen, Lynn M. *Women in Mathematics*. Cambridge, Mass.: MIT Press, 1974. Chapter on Sofia Kovalevskaia gives a good overview of her life and puts it in the perspective of changes in Russian and European society during the late 19th century.

Perl, Teri. *Women and Numbers*. San Carlos, California: Wide World Publishing/Tetra, 1993. This very readable book has a good chapter on Kovalevskaia.

Emmy Noether in her Bryn Mawr years. Considered a master of modern algebra, Noether moved to the United States when her name was placed on a Nazi "hit list." (Bryn Mawr College Archives)

Emmy Noether

(1882–1935)

Perhaps you have seen a picture of Albert Einstein. In the "classic" Einstein picture, the great physicist's expression seems intense, yet kindly. He doesn't seem to care much about his appearance—his white hair sticks out in all directions; his tie is rumpled and shoes scuffed.

Far fewer people have seen a picture of mathematician Emmy Noether, but she shared Einstein's intensity in many ways. Suffering from extreme nearsightedness, she peers intently through her powerful eyeglasses. Her hair slowly comes undone as she marches up and down in front of the blackboard writing formulas and diagrams. And nothing—not even a stubborn old professor or a Nazi storm trooper—could stop Emmy Noether. Her mathematical breakthroughs provided tools that Einstein and the later quantum physicists could use to study the mysterious particles within the atom.

Amalie Noether (Nur-thur) (usually called Emmy) was born in 1882 in the small German town of Erlangen. Her father, Max Noether, was a highly regarded mathematician who had done pioneering work in studying the rules underlying the workings of algebra.

For a Jewish family such as the Noethers, the late 19th century in Germany was a good time. The high regard for learning that is part of Jewish culture seemed to fit in well with the needs of the growing universities of Germany and with the public's admiration for scientists. Anti-Jewish feeling was at a low ebb.

Emmy grew up listening to lively mathematical discussions between her father and visiting mathematicians. Despite this exposure to mathematics, however, Emmy's early training was the standard kind given to well-bred girls. She learned how to cook and keep house. She also took piano lessons. Although she showed little ability in music, she did enjoy dancing.

Emmy also liked languages. She studied French and English in high school. After high school, she passed a test that certified her for teaching these languages in schools for girls. Having learned the "social graces" and having been equipped with a way to earn a living if need be, Emmy had achieved as much education as girls were expected to have. But Emmy's brother Fritz had gone to college, preparing to follow their father's career path in mathematics. Emmy decided that she, too, would study mathematics at the university.

German attitudes toward women in higher education had changed only a little since Sofia Kovalevskaia's time. Traditionalists fought hard to keep women out of the universities. At the University of Erlangen where Emmy wanted to study, the faculty senate had declared in 1898 that the admission of women would "overthrow all academic order."

But one small concession had been made toward women: They could attend lectures if the professor granted permission. From 1900 to 1902 Noether attended lectures at Erlangen. During the winter semester of 1903–1904, Noether visited the University of Göttingen, where she was able to hear lectures by the astronomer Karl Schwartzchild and top-notch mathematicians such as Felix Klein, Hermann Minkowski, and David Hilbert. It was an exciting time in science: The next year, an unknown Swiss civil service official named Albert Einstein would publish three papers that would lay the foundation for modern physics.

In 1907, Noether received her doctoral degree at Erlangen, "with highest honors." She now faced the same problem that Kovalevskaia had experienced a generation earlier: No one would give a woman a position teaching mathematics at a university. Noether had to settle for an unpaid job as a researcher at the Mathematical Institute at Erlangen, where she sometimes lectured in place of her father, whose health was beginning to fail.

Despite the lack of financial support, Noether did important work from 1908 to 1919. During this time Felix Klein and David Hilbert became interested in the mathematical underpinnings of Einstein's new theory of relativity. In particular, Einstein's equations often used quantities called *invariants*. (An invariant, or constant, is a value that does not change when certain operations are performed on it. In Einstein's theory of relativity, the speed of light is an invariant: It is always the same, regardless of how it is measured.) When they found that Emmy Noether, too, had started working on invariants, they invited her to work with them. She soon became indispensable. In a letter to Hilbert, Klein noted: "You know that it is [Emmy] Noether who is continually advising me in my projects, and that it is really through her that I have become competent in the subject." Hilbert in turn had mentioned "Emmy Noether, whom I called upon to help me with such questions as my theory on the conservation of energy." Later, Weyl wrote that "for two of the most significant sides of the theory of relativity, [Noether] gave at that time the genuine and universal mathematical formulation."

Despite her growing reputation, Noether's career remained blocked. To become a *Privatdozent*, or certified lecturer, required more than just a doctor's degree. The candidate had to go through a process called "habilitation" that included a special examination. A 1908 law had forbidden the habilitation of women, and one traditionalist asked "How can it be allowed that a woman become a Privatdozent? Having become a Privatdozent, she can then become a professor and a member of the University Senate. . . . What will our soldiers think when they return to the University and find that they are expected to learn at the feet of a woman?" While the non-mathematicians on the faculty tended to oppose Noether's appointment, the mathematicians, well acquainted with the value of her work, mainly supported her. David Hilbert stood up at one University Senate meeting and declared in an exasperated voice: "Gentlemen, I do not see that the sex of the candidate is an argument against her admission as a Privatdozent. After all, the Senate is not a bathhouse."

Despite Hilbert's efforts, Noether was not admitted as a Privatdozent. Instead, Hilbert set things up so that she could lecture under his name. When World War I ended in 1919, the new German republic had a somewhat more enlightened attitude toward women. In 1922, Noether was given the title

In a memorial speech after Emmy Noether's death in 1935, Herman Weyl said:

"She was not clay, pressed by the artistic hands of God into a harmonious form, but rather a chunk of human primary rock into which he had blown his creative breath of life."

of "unofficial associate professor," a position with no formal duties and no salary. A bit later she was finally given a small salary for teaching algebra.

During the 1920s Noether began to focus on the study of abstract algebra. Regular algebra—the kind taught in high school—is a generalization of arithmetic. That is, algebra uses letter symbols such as X, Y, and Z to stand as general "placeholders" for particular numbers. Generalization is a very powerful idea because it means that a single formula or equation can be used to solve any number of practical problems. For example, once you know that $V = {}^D/_T$ where V is velocity, D is distance, and T is time, you can, once given the appropriate data, find the velocity of an Olympic runner, a racing car, or a supersonic jet.

Abstract algebra is a further generalization. Instead of using particular equations or formulas, it starts with "groups" of numbers or other items. A group is like the sets of numbers that Georg Cantor studied. Groups can be classified according to the operations that can be performed on the items within them. For example, in the set of real numbers (integers, fractions, and irrational numbers), you can multiply any two or more numbers together and always get another number that is also part of the set of real numbers. Further, multiplication obeys certain laws. For any two numbers A and B, A × B = B × A (for example, 5 × 3 = 3 × 5; both are 15). This is called the commutative law of multiplication. And if you have three numbers A, B, and C, you can multiply A × B and then multiply the result by C, or you can multiply B × C and then multiply by A. In other words, (A × B) × C is the same as A × (B × C). This is called the associative law.

There are stranger-looking groups of numbers that also obey some of these laws. For example, you may have done "clock arithmetic" in school. In clock arithmetic, the set of numbers goes 1, 2, 3 and so on up to 12, and then back to 1 again, as on a clock dial. If it is 5:00 and eight hours pass, it doesn't become 13:00: it becomes 1:00. Thus in clock arithemtic, 5 + 8 is 1. But as with regular arithmetic, A + B = B + A by the commutative law. In clock arithmetic, 5 + 8 = 8 + 5; both are 1.

In 1921 Noether wrote an important paper with the title "Theory of Ideals in Rings." A *ring* is a special kind of set or group of items that obey certain commutative, associative, and other laws. (The set of real numbers is actually a ring). This paper was very general and abstract. As noted by mathematician Martha K. Smith, Noether "saw the connections between things that people hadn't realized were connected before. She was able to describe in a unified manner many ideas that people had thought were different. She saw their underlying similarity."

The most important application of Noether's work on rings was in physics. It turns out that rules like those that apply to groups of numbers can also be applied to groups of the particles that make up atoms. Just as equations such as A + B = B + A show symmetry (a pair of mirror images) in the realm of numbers, so, too, are there laws of symmetry in the way certain pairs of sub-atomic particles behave. And just as there are kinds of invariance in the number system, so, too, are there invariances in the physical system. (One example of an invariance is the law of conservation of energy and matter. This law says that no matter what operation you perform on a physical system over a period of time, the total amount of energy and matter will remain the same. Only the form or distribution will change.) There are other kinds of conservation in physics as well, and Noether showed that each kind of conservation has a corresponding symmetry. This means that if you know about either the conservation or the symmetry in a given case, you can eventually work out the other side of the picture.

Noether's years at Göttingen were very important in the development of modern mathematics. Her students would become world-class experts in ring theory, number theory, and other areas. One student, B. L. van der Waerden, wrote a book that popularized Noether's ideas in America. The eventual result was the "New Math," an approach to mathematics education that emphasized general mathematical concepts over the doing of rote problems.

Noether had become internationally famous. In the winter of 1924–1925, she taught at the University of Moscow and inspired a new generation of Soviet mathematicians. In 1932, Noether won a mathematics prize and then became the only woman to have ever addressed a general session of the International Congress of Mathematics in Zurich, Switzerland.

A few months later, however, Adolf Hitler and his Nazi Party came to power in Germany. One of Hitler's first actions was to order the firing of Jewish professors in the universities. Noether was a Jew, a pacifist, and a believer in liberal political ideas. Her name, along with that of five other professors at Göttingen, was on the very first target list. Noether's students petitioned the government to allow her to stay, but nothing could be done.

After Noether's death, Albert Einstein summed up the importance of her work as follows:

"In the judgement of the most competent living mathematicians, Fraulein Noether was the most significant creative mathematical genius thus far produced since the higher education of women began. In the realm of algebra in which the most gifted mathematicians have been busy for centuries, she discovered methods which have proved of enormous importance in the development of the present day younger generation of mathematicians."

Noether responded to Nazi attacks with her characteristic energy and directness. Together with Weyl, she helped start a German Mathematical Relief Fund to help the Jewish mathematicians who had lost their jobs. Forbidden to teach at the university, she continued classes in her apartment. Weyl later remembered how

> her courage, her frankness, her unconcern about her own fate, her conciliatory [peace-making] spirit were, in the midst of all the hatred and meanness and despair, and sorrow surrounding us, a moral solace. . . . Her heart knew no malice; she did not believe in evil—indeed it never entered her mind that it could play a role among men.

But time was running out. Noether's friends stepped up their efforts to find jobs abroad for Jewish mathematicians like Noether. After considering several possibilities, Noether secured a job offer from Bryn Mawr, a prestigious women's college in Philadelphia, Pennsylvania. When Noether came to America, she found her way eased by Anna Pell Wheeler, a well-known American mathematician who had studied at Göttingen and was familiar with German culture. They quickly became friends. Noether's students at Bryn Mawr were inspired by the challenge of her rapid-fire lectures, filled with a mixture of English and German terms.

Noether seemed to adjust well to life in America, but she was disturbed by the continuing destruction of science and culture in Germany at the hands of the Nazis. She also worried about getting a suitable permanent position. Her teaching at Bryn Mawr was supported by a temporary fellowship, and involved teaching undergraduate students, while Noether really wanted to do research and only teach a few graduate students. A possible position at the Institute for Advanced Studies at Princeton (where Albert Einstein had moved some years earlier) offered the best hope for Noether's future.

Noether had been suffering from growths in her uterus, or womb. On April 10, 1935, she had surgery to remove an ovarian cyst. Her recovery from the operation seemed to be normal, but on the fourth day she suddenly lost consciousness, suffered a raging fever, and died, probably from an infection. Like Sofia Kovalevskaia, Emmy Noether had been cut down unexpectedly at the height of her creative powers.

In 1982, on the 100th anniversary of Emmy Noether's birth, the Association of Women in Mathematics had a special symposium in her honor. Paying her belated tribute, the city of Erlangen named a high school after her.

Chronology

March 23, 1882	Emmy Noether born in Erlangen, Bavaria, Germany
1900	begins to attend university lectures
1904	attends lectures at Göttingen; graduates from University of Erlangen
1905	Albert Einstein publishes papers on special relativity and the quantum theory of light

1907	Noether earns her doctoral degree at Erlangen with highest honors
1908–1915	works as unpaid researcher at Mathematical Institute in Erlangen; works on theory of invariants
1914–1919	World War I leads to upheaval in Germany
1921	Noether publishes paper on ring theory
1922	gets title of "unofficial associate professor" without salary
1922–1932	becomes an internationally famous mathematician
1932	Wins mathematics prize; becomes only woman ever to address general session of the International Congress of Mathematics in Zurich, Switzerland
1933	Nazis come to power; Noether moves to Bryn Mawr college in Philadelphia
April 14, 1935	Noether dies unexpectedly following surgery

Further Reading

Brewer, James W., and Martha K. Smith. *Emmy Noether: A Tribute to Her Life and Work.* New York: Marcel Dekker, Inc., 1981. The first part of this book is a biography of Noether and a discussion of her influence on mathematics.

McGrayne, Sharon Bertsch. *Nobel Prize Women in Science: Their Lives, Struggles, and Momentous Discoveries.* New York: Carol Publishing Group, 1993. This book includes a good biographical chapter on Noether.

Perl, Teri. *Women and Numbers*. San Carlos, California: World Wide Publishing/Tetra, 1993. Chapter on Emmy Noether provides a good, brief introduction to her life. Activities illustrate the mathematical concepts of operations on groups.

Srinivasa Ramanujan. This young Indian mathematician astonished the experts of Europe with dazzling theorems in number theory. It was said that "every natural number was his personal friend." (Master and fellows of Trinity College, Cambridge)

Srinivasa Ramanujan

(1887–1920)

Godfrey Harold Hardy was probably the greatest British mathematician of the early 20th century. He was witty, learned, and masterful. A lifelong fan of the English bat-and-ball game called cricket, Hardy was what the English used to call "a scholar and a gentleman." Working at the famous Trinity College of Cambridge University, Hardy had been largely responsible for teaching British students about the new European developments that were revolutionizing mathematics in the early 20th century.

Mathematics seemed indeed to be a monopoly of Europeans. Historians knew that some of the most important basic mathematical ideas (such as the "Arabic" numerals and the zero) had originally come from India, but few Europeans were looking for contributions to modern mathematics from other continents.

One day in January, 1913, however, Hardy was sorting through his mail. His eyes were drawn by a large envelope covered with stamps from India. The envelope was stuffed with sheets of paper, topped by a letter. The letter read:

Dear Sir,

I beg to introduce myself to you as a clerk in the Accounts Department of the Port Trust Office at Madras on a salary of only 20 [pounds] per annum. I am now about 23 years of age. I have had no University education but I have undergone the ordinary school course. After leaving school I have been employing the spare time at my disposal to work at Mathematics. I have not trodden through the conventional regular course which is followed in a University course, but I am striking out on a new path for myself. I have made a special investigation of divergent series in general and the results I get are termed by the local mathematicians as "startling."

The writer, Srinivasa Ramanujan (Shrin´-i-vas-uh Rah´-mah-noo-jen), then made specific claims that he had solved a variety of mathematical problems. For example, he said that he had found a formula that could provide a very accurate estimate of how many prime numbers came before a given number. (A prime number is a number that can be divided only by itself and 1. For example, 3, 5, and 7 are prime numbers; 9 is not a prime number, since it can be divided by 3.) Hardy himself had been trying to find such a formula. Now this unknown young man from India was insisting that he could do better than England's greatest mathematicians.

The formulas went on for page after page, densely packed with number series, complicated repeated fractions, and heavy-duty calculus. At first, Hardy assumed that the letter was the work of a crank. After all, famous scientists and mathematicians were used to receiving letters containing diagrams of perpetual-motion machines or elaborate geometrical proofs that contained elementary errors.

Hardy put the letter aside, but something kept nagging at him. He invited a fellow mathematician, John Littlewood, to look over Ramanujan's formulas with him. They found that some of the formulas were the same as ones they already knew. Others turned out to be different ways of expressing familiar ideas. But many of the formulas were like nothing they had seen before. Hardy and Littlewood were intrigued by the work of the unkown Indian mathematician.

Srinivasa Ramanujan had come from a far different upbringing than that of Hardy and his colleagues from elite schools. Srinivasa was born in the town of Erode in South India in 1887. (In keeping with Indian custom, his first name, Srinivasa, was simply the first name of his father, Srinivasa Iyengar.) India was a British colony, and the government and educational system were organized along British lines. Srinivasa's father was a clerk in a fabric shop, and the family lived in reasonable comfort.

Srinivasa was a "slow" child at first. He didn't speak until he was three years old. Once he started talking, however, he showed his curiosity by asking endless questions. In elementary school he did very well; at the age of ten he had the highest examination scores in the district and went directly to high school. In high school, his mathematical abilities became evident to everyone.

One day a teacher was showing the class how any number divided by itself was one. If three people divided three fruits, he said, each person would get one. If a thousand people divided a thousant fruits, each person would still get one fruit. Srinivasa then spoke up: "But is zero divided by zero also one? If no fruits are divided among no one, will each still get one?" His question, in fact, could not be answered yes or no. The number system breaks down if you try to divide by zero, so mathematicians say that division by zero is undefined.

Srinivasa was especially intrigued by number series. A number series is a list of numbers that shows some sort of pattern. For example, the series 2, 4, 6, . . . represents the even numbers from 2 to infinity. Each number (2, 4, and so on) is called a *term* of the series. The series of even numbers isn't particularly interesting: The total of its terms is clearly infinite, since there are an infinite number of even numbers, each two more than the previous one.

Series made from fractions have more interesting properties. For example, consider the series $1 + \frac{1}{2} + \frac{1}{3} + \frac{1}{4} + \frac{1}{5}$ . . . . If you add up the first four numbers you get a total greater than 2 (about 2.083). As you continue to add numbers, the total increases more and more slowly because each successive fraction is smaller and smaller. (The first 10 terms add up to about 2.93, the first 100 to 5.18, the first 1,000 to 7.49, and even the first 10,000 haven't even reached 10 yet, being about 9.79. Because this series never stops increasing, it is called *divergent*.

Nowadays, it's easy to plug a formula into a computer and add up as many terms of a series as you want. Srinivasa Ramanujan didn't have a computer, and he had to do his arithmetic by hand. In fact, one time, when a friend said "Ramanuju, they call you a genius," he replied, "Look at my elbow. That will tell you the story." His elbow was almost black. He did his calculations on a slate, and he had found that it was faster to erase old numbers with his elbow than to use a rag. He used the worn slate because he had no money to buy paper.

But while calculation has its place, discoveries in number theory come mainly from intuition, or the ability to see hidden patterns. Consider the series $1 + \frac{1}{3} + \frac{1}{6} + \frac{1}{10} + \frac{1}{15} + \frac{1}{21}$ . . . . In this series, each fraction has a numerator of 1 and a denominator that consists of the sum of the whole numbers up to that term. For example, the third term, $\frac{1}{6}$, is equal to $\frac{1}{(1+2+3)}$, the fourth term, $\frac{1}{10}$, is $\frac{1}{(1+2+3+4)}$, and so on.

What does this series add up to? If you use a computer (or a lot of chalk), you can find that the first 5 terms add up to 1.667; the first 10 to 1.818, the first 100 to 1.980, and the first 1,000 to 1.998. In fact, the more terms you add, the closer the total comes to 2—though, like Zeno's Achilles, it never quite gets there.

But someone as creative as young Srinivasa didn't have to add up the numbers. He would see that the series $1 + \frac{1}{3} + \frac{1}{6} + \frac{1}{10} + \frac{1}{15} + \frac{1}{21} \ldots$ was the same as $2 \times (\frac{1}{2} + \frac{1}{6} + \frac{1}{12} + \frac{1}{20} + \frac{1}{30} \ldots)$. He would then see that each fraction could be expressed as a difference between two other fractions: For example, $\frac{1}{2} = 1 - \frac{1}{2}$; $\frac{1}{6} = \frac{1}{2} - \frac{1}{3}$; $\frac{1}{12} = \frac{1}{3} - \frac{1}{4}$, and so on. He would then rewrite the series as $2 \times [(1 - \frac{1}{2}) + (\frac{1}{2} - \frac{1}{3}) + (\frac{1}{3} - \frac{1}{4}) + (\frac{1}{4} - \frac{1}{5}) \ldots)$. And when you cancel out the $-\frac{1}{2}$ and $\frac{1}{2}$ (which add up to 0); the $-\frac{1}{3}$ and $+\frac{1}{3}$, and so on, you get a result of $2 \times (1 - 0) = 2 \times 1 = 2$. In other words, you can prove that this infinite series adds up to 2 without actually adding the terms.

The branch of mathematics called number theory is filled with patterns, puzzles, and interesting questions about series and sums. Srinivasa spent hours playing with numbers in this way, but then he found a more systematic introduction to mathematics.

Just before graduating from high school, a visiting college student lent Srinivasa a book. Its title was *A Synopsis of Results in Pure and Applied Mathematics*. The author, George Shoobridge Carr, had compiled a kind of master outline of all the fundamental theorems and formulas of algebra, geometry, trigonometry, and calculus. The book laid everything out in order, but did not offer detailed proofs. In a classroom in England, the teacher would probably spend an hour demonstrating each theorem, step by step. Srinivasa had only this one book. It captivated him, and he devoured page after page, working out the proofs as he went along.

Unfortunately, Ramanujan was so absorbed by his study of mathematics that when he went to the district's Government College in 1904, he walked through his courses and lectures as though in a dream. While a lecturer went over a point in ancient history or biology, likely as not Ramanjun was constructing "magic squares" in his head. (A magic square is a grid of numbers where all the rows, columns, and diagonals add up to the same total.) Prime numbers, series, and fractions occupied most of his waking hours. As a result, Ramanujan flunked his college courses. Two years later, at another college in Madras, the same thing happened. Ramanujan was brilliant in his mathematics courses and often left his teachers far behind. But since he paid no attention to his other courses, he lost his scholarship.

In a way, Ramanujan was saved by his mother Komalatammal. In 1908, she encountered a young woman named Janaki who was the daughter of a distant relative. In India, marriages were usually arranged by the parents. Janaki was only eight years old, but it was common for children to be married in childhood—they would live together when they grew up. Komalatammal asked for a copy of Janaki's horoscope, examined it, and decided that the young woman would be a compatible mate for her son. Srinivasa and Janaki were married on July 14, 1909. Marriage meant that in the eyes of Indian society Ramanujan was no longer a youth, but a responsible householder. Social obligations forced him to put aside mathematics to find a job.

Hardy, looking back at Ramanujan's work, wrote:

"There is always more in one of Ramanujan's formulae than meets the eye, as anyone who sets to work to verify those which look the easiest will soon discover. In some the interest lies very deep, in others comparatively near the surface; but there is not one which is not curious and entertaining."

One person whom Ramanujan approached was V. Ramaswami Ayer. Ayer was a government official, but he was also a mathematician who had just founded the Indian Mathematical Society. He later said that when Ramanujan showed him his notebook, "I was struck by the extraordinary mathematical results contained in it." He didn't give Ramanujan a job, but he gave him a letter of reference to colleagues in Madras. These included R. Ramachandra Rao, who was a noted mathematician and a person who had many business and social connections.

Rao had trouble understanding Ramanujan's notebooks, and at first, he suspected him of fraud. Finally, though, he realized that the young man was a genuine mathematical genius. Rao paid Ramanujan's living expenses for a few months. Meanwhile, Ramanujan wrote a paper about Bernoulli numbers, which are defined using infinite series. An important part of these series was a "magic number" called e. e can be defined as the sum of the series $1 + {}^1/_{1!} + {}^1/_{2!} + {}^1/_{3!} + {}^1/_{4!} \ldots$ where the exclamation point in the denominators of the fractions means to take the factorial, multiplying all the numbers between one and that number together. For example, factorial 4, or 4! is equal to $1 \times 2 \times 3 \times 4$, or 24. The paper was accepted by the *Journal of the Indian Mathematical Society*, and it marked the formal entrance of Ramanujan into the world of mathematicians.

Ramanujan still needed a regular job. Finally, in 1912, Rao found him a position as a clerk with the port of Madras. While working took away time from mathematics, Ramanujan's life now had some stability. In 1913, he wrote his letter to Hardy in England. The mathematical samples that Ramanujan included with his letter intrigued Hardy. Hardy knew that if they proved to be true, they were tremendously valuable. Ramanujan offered no actual proof of most of his statements. When Hardy replied to Ramanujan's letter, he was very generous in his praise for the talent Ramanujan had shown. But he also asked for proof for the new theorems—the step-by-step demonstration that a new conclusion actually followed from things already known to be true.

Ramanujan did not humbly agree to Hardy's demands, however. In a return letter, he replied ". . . you will not be able to follow my methods of proof if I indicate the lines on which I proceed in a single letter. You may ask how you can accept results based on wrong premises. What I tell you is this: Verify the results I give and if they agree with your results, got by treading on the groove in which the present day mathematicians move, you should at least grant that there may be some truths in my fundamental basis."

Ramanujan was no longer shy about asking for help. In writing to Hardy, he also said that "I am already a half-starving man. To preserve brains I want [need] food and this is now my first consideration. Any sympathetic letter from you will be helpful to me here to get a scholarship either from the University or from Government."

Hardy and Ramanujan's friends went to work raising the necessary funds. In 1914, Ramanujan sailed for England. Now Hardy and Ramanujan could work together. The result would be some of the most bold and imaginative papers in modern number theory. For example, while mathematicians had worked with prime numbers since ancient Greek times, no one until Ramanujan had thought to look at the kind of numbers that were the very opposite of prime—numbers that had many divisors. Ramanujan called these numbers "highly composite numbers." (An example is 24, which has eight divisors: 1, 2, 3, 4, 6, 8, 12, and 24 itself.)

Another paper explored the idea of "partitions." Partitions express the different ways that integers can be added together to form a given total. For example, the partitions of 4 would be 1+1+1+1, 2+2, 1+3, and 0 + 4. Ramanujan developed a formula that could predict with great accuracy

how many partitions a number such as 50 might have (the answer is very many—204,226 to be exact).

Hardy and Ramanujan made an excellent team. For all of his brilliance, Ramanujan had not had a systematic education in mathematics. While Ramanujan could churn out state-of-the-art equations, Hardy found that "the limits of his knowledge were as startling as its profundity [depth]." Ramanujan lacked knowledge about some things taught to beginning college students. Hardy was able to fill in some of the gaps in Ramanujan's knowledge without frustrating or irritating him.

Further, Ramanujan often used flashes of intuition to find his startlingly original ideas. Publishing these ideas in papers required that they be proven step by step, and Ramanujan did not know how to do this very well. Here, too, Hardy supplied the missing ingredient.

In the years following 1914, Ramanujan was quite productive. But the outbreak of World War I had cut mathematicians in England off from their colleagues in Germany and other European nations. Just when he would most benefit from meeting many international mathematicians, Ramanujan was denied the opportunity. Further, he soon began to miss his native land. Ramanujan, like most Hindus, was a vegetarian. The war made fresh vegetables scarce. Lonely and homesick, Ramanujan also began to suffer serious health problems. In particular, it was found that he had tuberculosis, a lung disease that was incurable until an antibiotic that killed the TB

Hardy went to see Ramanujan in the hospital. To make conversation, he remarked that the number of the cab he came in, 1729, wasn't very interesting. Ramanujan disagreed:

"It's a very interesting number. It's the smallest number expressible as the sum of two cubes in two different ways — $1^3 + 12^3$ and $9^3 + 10^3$."

bacteria was invented a generation later.

In 1919, Ramanujan returned to India. His poor health made it difficult for him to do mathematical work. He died on April 26, 1920, at the age of 32.

Ever since Ramanujan's death, mathematicians have studied his notebooks. Scientists have found applications of his mathematics in fields as different as chemistry, cancer treatment, and computer programming. (The supercomputers that calculated the number pi to more than a billion decimal places in the late 1980s used algorithms, or rules of calculation, that are based in part on Ramanujan's paper on the aproximation of pi.)

Ramanujan's life brings up the classic question about any genius who died young. What might he have been able to accomplish if he had lived even another 10 years? What we do know is that Ramanujan broadened the horizons of mathematics and showed that they reached beyond Europe.

Chronology

December 22, 1887	Srinivasa Ramanujan born in Erode, India
1903	reads Carr's *Synopsis* and plunges into mathematical exploration
1903–1907	absorbed with mathematics, fails college twice
July 14, 1909	marries Janaki, begins to seek employment
1910–1912	shows his work to Indian mathematicians; gets a clerical job
1913	writes to G. H. Hardy at Cambridge
1914	goes to England; begins to write major papers

1918	elected Fellow of the Royal Society and awarded Fellowship of Trinity College, Cambridge
1919	returns to India in ill health
April 26, 1920	dies in Madras, India of tuberculosis

Further Reading

Borwein, Jonathan M., and Peter B. Borwein. "Ramanujan and Pi" in Ferris, Timothy, ed. *The World Treasury of Physics, Astronomy, and Mathematics*. Discusses Ramanujan's part in the search for ever more accurate representations of the number pi, a "magic number" that turns up in many parts of mathematics.

Hardy, G. H. *A Mathematician's Apology*. Cambridge: Cambridge University Press, 1940 (reprinted 1967). Includes Hardy's account of his work with Ramanujan and life at Oxford in the early 20th century.

Kanigel, Robert. *The Man Who Knew Infinity: A Life of the Genius Ramanujan.* New York: Washington Square Press, 1991. A superb popular biography of Ramanujan.

Paulos, John Allen. *Beyond Numeracy*. New York: Vintage Books, 1992. The chapter "Series—Convergence and Divergence" introduces some simple number series of the kind that intrigued Ramanujan as a youngster.

Stanislaw Ulam had a gift for visualizing physical processes. In 1943, he found himself working in a secret atomic bomb project. Later, he found ways to use computers to mirror reality. (Reprinted from *I Have a Photographic Memory* by Paul R. Halmos, by permission of the American Mathematical Society)

Stanislaw Ulam

(1909–1984)

The year was 1943, and the world was in the midst of the greatest war in history. Stanislaw Ulam, a mathematician at the University of Wisconsin, wanted to help the Allies win the war against Hitler. Ulam, a researcher in pure mathematics, wasn't sure what use set theory or probability and statistics might be in the war effort. He had, however, received an invitation from physicist Hans Bethe to work on a project that seemed to have something to do with studying the physics of what goes on inside stars.

He wrote to his friend, the great mathematician and computer pioneer John von Neumann, and asked him what this was all about. Von Neumann's answer was equally vague:

> The project in question is exceedingly important, . . . It is very interesting and the theoretical (and other) physicists connected with it are probably the best group existing anywhere at the moment.
>
> The secrecy requirements of this project are rather extraordinary. It will probably necessitate your and your families essentially staying on the premises (except for vacations) as long as you choose to be associated with it.

> Ulam still had no idea what the project was all about, but the chance of working with world-class physicists on a mysterious problem was hard to resist. Ulam packed his bags and eventually found himself in the midst of a city of barbed wire, shacks, and two-story wooden buildings rising in the desert near Santa Fe, New Mexico. It was called the Manhattan Project, and Ulam and his colleagues were being asked to design the first atomic bomb.

Stanislaw Ulam was born in Lvov, Poland, in 1909. His parents were part of a family of well-to-do Jewish bankers, and Stanislaw was able to take advantage of the best tutors and schools. When he was 10 years old his interest in science awakened: first astronomy, then physics, and finally, mathematics. At the age of 12 he amazed visiting relatives with his explanations of Einstein's theory of relativity, which was the hot new topic in science at the time. By the time he was fifteen and in high school, Stanislaw was reading books on number theory.

One problem that intrigued Stanislaw had to do with perfect numbers. A perfect number is a number whose factors or divisors (counting 1 but not counting the number itself) add up to that number. For example, 28 is a perfect number because its divisors are $1 + 2 + 4 + 7 + 14 = 28$. Perfect numbers are few and far between—and all the known ones are even. Ulam wondered whether there could be a perfect number that was odd. To this day, no one knows the answer.

In 1927, Ulam entered the Lvov Polytechnic Institute. Since he knew that there would be few positions available in pure mathematics, he entered the engineering course, although he chose as many mathematics courses as possible. During the time Ulam was in college, Polish mathematicians such as Stefan Banach, Kazamir Kuratowski, and Stanislaw

Mazur were doing internationally famous work in fields such as topology (the study of shapes) and set theory. Ulam soon impressed his teachers with the way he tackled difficult problems. But an equally important part of his education came after classes, when he and other students gathered at the oddly named Scottish Cafe to brainstorm mathematical problems over coffee and brandy.

By the time Ulam received his undergraduate degree, he had switched from engineering to pure mathematics. Today mathematics, like most of the sciences, is highly specialized. After taking introductory courses, the student soon has to specialize in one particular field. Ulam, however, started his career in the 1930s, when it was still possible for one person to do useful research in several different fields of mathematics. He explored set and group theory, where the system built by Georg Cantor in the previous century was being challenged by new ideas—especially Kurt Godel's proof in 1931 that any mathematical system was necessarily incomplete—that is, that it contained things that could not be proved using the rules of that system. Ulam's work in fields as different as topology and probability theory (dealing with the chances of certain things happening) would come together in surprising ways in his later work in Los Alamos.

Ulam spent 1934 touring some of the great universities of Europe and studying at Vienna, Zurich, Paris, and Cambridge. Hitler had just come to power, however, and the shadow of Nazism had begun to loom over Europe. Along with other Jewish mathematicians such as Emmy Noether, Ulam began to seek a position outside of Europe. He wrote to John von Neumann at Harvard University in the United States. Von Neumann had heard of Ulam's work and he invited him to visit. When they met, they found that they shared a common Jewish culture and a lively sense of humor. With the help of von Neumann and other friends at Harvard, Ulam obtained a fellowship.

From 1936 to 1939 Ulam worked during the school year at Harvard and visited Poland during the summer. Just after the last summer, however, German tanks and bombers suddenly attacked Poland, and World War II began. "At that moment," Ulam recalls, "I suddenly felt as if a curtain had fallen on my past life. . . . There has been a different color and meaning to everything ever since."

When his Harvard fellowship ended, Ulam went to the University of Wisconsin at Madison. While teaching there, he met and married Francoise Aron. They settled down happily, but the pleasant routine of academic life would be interrupted by the entry of the United States into the war and the invitation to Los Alamos and the Manhattan Project.

When he arrived at Los Alamos, Ulam recalls, "They were talking about things which I only vaguely understood. There were tremendously long formulae on the blackboard, which scared me. . . . . However, when day after day the same equations remained and were not changed every few hours as I expected, I regained my confidence and some hope of being able to add something to the theoretical work."

At Los Alamos, Ulam was the only pure mathematician in a group that consisted mainly of physicists. Ulam discovered that mathematicians and physicists tend to look at problems from opposite ends: "Mathematicians start with certain facts—which we call axioms—and deduce consequences. In physics, in a sense, it's the other way around: The physicists have a lot of facts, lots of relations, formal expressions, which are the results of experiments; and they search for a small number of simple laws—we could call them axioms in this case—from which these [experimental] results can be deduced."

Ulam had to rush to familiarize himself with the details of nuclear reactions, but when he did, he found that he, like the creative young physicist Richard Feynman, had the kind of intuition that enabled him to visualize a physical process and come up with a "seat of the pants" calculation that could quickly tell him whether his thinking was going in the right direction.

Ulam found that his previous work in sets, groups, and probability made it possible for him to develop new mathematical tools to aid the bomb designers. In nuclear fission, neutrons bombard heavy atoms of uranium or plutonium, splitting them and releasing energy and more neutrons that in turn can split other atoms. The key problem is to design the bomb in such a way that enough neutrons hit enough atoms quickly enough to produce an out-of-control fission reaction—a nuclear explosion.

Ulam realized that the nuclear reaction was an example of the "branching processes" that he had begun to study a few years earlier. He noted that "at each stage of the process, there are many possibilities determining the fate of the neutron. It can scatter at one angle, change its velocity, be absorbed, or produce more neutrons by a fission of the target nucleus, and so on." Physicists could estimate the probability of each of these branches, or outcomes, but it would be very difficult to write equations that could show what would happen after thousands or even millions of collisions had taken place—each one creating a new set of possibilities.

So Ulam didn't attempt such a calculation. Rather, he used the physicists' knowledge of probabilities to "roll the dice" by selecting a random number for a particle. The probabilities would determine what happened to that particle, and then the dice wold be rolled again. Eventually, the simulated particles would form a

Ulam was asked to say whether he was satisfied with the consequences of his work on the atomic bomb at Los Alamos.

"It's hard to say—satisfied from what point of view? It's hard to say, certainly, 'satisfied' or 'dissatisfied' with the facts of nature. These things exist."

picture of how the actual physical process would turn out, given a certain set of starting conditions. Ulam later developed this approach into a general-purpose research tool called the Monte Carlo method. (Monte Carlo is a famous gambling casino and refers to the use of random numbers in the method.)

The methods Ulam pioneered are used today at the powerful computer work stations that have become a fixture in every laboratory. In the mid 1940s, however, the computer was in its infancy. Ulam and his friend John von Neumann urged that better computers such as MANIAC be developed to allow for the huge number of calculations needed for probability simulations. Ulam's work helped turn the computer from a glorified calculator to a powerful tool for exploring scientific ideas.

The scientists at Los Alamos argued about what would happen when the atomic bomb was set off. A few believed that the nuclear reaction would spread uncontrolled through the earth's atmosphere, ending life on earth. Ulam's calculations proved to be correct, however. On July 16, 1945, the world's first atomic explosion burst like a second sun on the horizon of a New Mexico desert. The explosion did not destroy the world—but it showed that the weapon could unleash incredible powers of destruction.

When the war ended, Ulam and the other scientists assumed that the Los Alamos lab would be shut down because there would be little need for weapons research. He started to look for another position. Unfortunately, working on a top secret bomb project meant that he hadn't added to the list of published papers that is an important measure of a scientist's ability. He missed the exhilarating collaboration with the world's best physicists at Los Alamos. Ulam could only find employment at the University of Southern California, and he felt depressed at the prospect that he would have to teach undergraduate mathematics courses instead of doing research.

To add to his problems, Ulam came down with encephalitis, a serious brain infection. When he recovered, he found that Los Alamos was hiring people after all. The Cold War had begun, and the United States and the Soviet Union were competing to build nuclear weapons. Ulam started working on a project that its leader, physicist Edward Teller, called "the super." This was the hydrogen fusion bomb, which worked by fusing, or bringing together, atoms. Looking at Teller's design for the trigger device that was supposed to start the fusion reaction, Ulam discovered that it would not work. He came up with an alternative design. But Ulam did not get along well with Teller, who had a domineering personality and seemed to be obsessed with the new bomb.

Ulam was more interested in peaceful uses of nuclear power. He even worked on a project that might have resulted in a nuclear-propelled spaceship that could explore the solar system. This project, called Orion, was eventually cancelled, however, because it required that the ship be propelled by a series of nuclear explosions as it flew through the earth's atmosphere.

Ulam maintained a working relationship with the Los Alamos lab, but during the 1950s and 1960s he taught and did research at a number of different universities. Until von Neumann's death in 1957, he worked closely with him on new

In the short span of my life great changes have taken place in the sciences . . . . Sometimes I feel that a more rational explanation for all that has happened during my lifetime is that I am still only thirteen years old, reading Jules Verne or H. G. Wells, and have fallen asleep.

—Stanislaw Ulam

mathematical techniques involving computers. One idea, called automata, used computer simulations where individual "cells" were made to live, die, or change according to a set of simple rules. Automata theory could be applied to a variety of complex systems including crystals and colonies of bacteria. (Automata will be discussed in more detail in the chapter on John Conway.)

Unlike many of the mathematicians discussed in this book, Stanislaw Ulam had a long and productive working life. He died at Santa Fe in 1984, at the age of 75. His most important achievements were in the way he bridged the gap between abstract mathematics and experimental physics, and in how he, together with von Neumann, showed how computer technology could be used to explore mathematical and scientific ideas.

Chronology

April 13, 1909	Stanislaw Ulam born in Lvov, Poland
1927	enters Lvov Polytechnic Institute
1928	writes his first mathematical paper
1933	gets doctorate from Polytechnic; shifts interest from engineering to mathematics
1936–1940	lectures at Harvard University
1941–1943	goes to University of Wisconsin; marries Francoise Aran
1943	receives invitation to join the atomic bomb project
1949	begins to work on the hydrogen bomb
1951–1957	works with John von Neumann on automata theory and computer simulation

1961–1983	serves as guest professor at several universities
May 13, 1984	Stanislaw Ulam dies

Further Reading

Albers, Donald J., and G. L. Alexanderson, eds. *Mathematical People: Profiles and Interiews*. Chicago: Contemporary Books, 1985. Includes an interview with Stanislaw Ulam.

Los Alamos Science. Special Issue, 1987. Devoted to a celebration of the life and work of Stanislaw Ulam. Shows the diversity of his work and his influence on modern mathematics and physics.

Ulam, Stanislaw M. *Adventures of a Mathematician*. New York: Charles Scribner's Sons, 1976. This is Ulam's autobiography and is quite readable.

Shiing-Shen Chern brought geometry back into the forefront of mathematical research. His "fiber bundle" geometry has formed the basis for theories about the fundamental forces of the universe. (Reprinted by permission of the American Mathematical Society)

Shiing-Shen Chern

(1911–)

You have probably studied some geometry in school. To the beginner, geometry seems to be mainly about lines and angles and the things that can be built from them—squares, rectangles, triangles, and so on. Some students find geometry easier to learn than algebra, because geometry at least starts with things you can see.

Later, the student learns that geometry and algebra can be two different ways of expressing the same mathematical truths. A line can be described by a simple algebraic equation. In turn, values can be plugged into an equation and the results plotted as a line on a graph.

Today's mathematicians have gone far beyond the geometry of lines and angles that was known to the ancient Greeks. Today there are several different kinds of geometries being explored by mathematicians, and each makes its own assumptions and draws its own logical conclusions. Some of the most advanced work in geometry has been done by a Chinese-American mathematician named Shiing-Shen Chern.

Shiing-Shen Chern was born on October 28, 1911, in Kashing, Chekiang Province, China. In what we could call junior high school today, Shiing-Shen took algebra (and advanced algebra), geometry, and trigonometry. When he was only 15 years old, he enrolled in Nankai University in Tientsin. He took some science courses, but he found he was clumsy at laboratory work. His problems in the lab and the presence of an excellent mathematics teacher, Dr. Li-fu Chiang, steered Chern toward a major in mathematics. Luckily, Chern had enrolled in one of the few universities in China that offered the more advanced types of mathematics, such as non-Euclidean and spherical geometry.

Indeed, Chern soon found that geometry was the part of mathematics that most interested him. In the classical, or Euclidean, geometry that Chern learned as a schoolboy, one of the fundamental postulates (or assumptions) is that if you have a line and a point outside that line, one and only one line can be drawn through the point that will be parallel to the first line. (One logical outcome of this assumption, called the parallel postulate, is that the sums of the angles within a triangle always add up to 180 degrees).

In the early 19th century, however, two mathematicians, the Hungarian Janos Bolyai and the Russian Nicolai Lobachevsky, showed that one could throw out Euclid's parallel postulate and come up with a strange yet logically consistent form of geometry. For example, suppose that your geometrical "world" consisted of a huge sphere rather than an endless flat plane. In the spherical world, "straight" lines are actually curved, following a "great circle" like that flown by an airliner going from Europe over the north pole and down into Asia. In this form of geometry (called elliptic geometry) there is no such thing as parallel lines, and the angles within a triangle add up to more than 180 degrees.

When non-Euclidean geometry was first proposed in the early 19th century, most people thought it was little more than a curiosity; the real world, after all, did seem to have parallel lines and straight triangles. But in the early 20th century Einstein's new physics said that space (and thus all lines) were actually curved. Because the universe is so large, the curvature is very slight—but it turned out that Einstein's physics needed non-Euclidean geometry. Later, Chern would make geometrical discoveries that would help modern physicists.

After graduation from Nankai, Chern entered the graduate school at Tsing Hua University in Peking. His most important teacher there, Dan Sun, specialized in something called projective differential geometry. Projective geometry takes figures (such as triangles) and "projects" them on a different surface in much the way an object lit by the sun casts a shadow. The triangular marker on a sundial can cast a shadow that is longer but is still a triangle.

As mathematicians studied different kinds of geometry (Euclidean, spherical, projective, and so on) they asked: What changes about this circle, or line, or triangle? And what remains the same? Chern read many papers on projective geometry, and began to write some of his own.

In 1934, Chern received a fellowship for study in the United States, but, because he had heard of the work of Wilhelm Blaschke, a well-known geometer, Chern managed to rearrange things so that he could go to the University of Hamburg in Germany instead. Chern attended some lectures by another noted mathematician, Emil Artin, on algebra and number theory. He said that the lectures were done so beautifully that he was tempted to switch to algebra, but his love of geometry won out.

Chern then went to Paris to study differential geometry with Elie Cartan. (Differential geometry applies the equations of calculus to points on a geometrical figure, such as a curve. The equations show how the curvature is changing at a particular point, and the equations can be "built up" into a more general picture of the figure's geometrical characteristics.) Cartan was a world leader in this kind of geometry, but his papers were considered to be very difficult to understand. Soon, however, Chern and Cartan were meeting after class and discussing problems together.

In the summer of 1937, Chern was ready to return to China, where he hoped to contribute to the growth of Chinese mathematics at Tsing Hua University. But while he was still aboard ship, Japan began its all-out war against China. Several major Chinese universities relocated to the city of Changsha and then to Kunming to stay ahead of the advancing Japanese troops. For about six years Chern carried on his teaching under difficult conditions, isolated by the war from the mathematicians of Europe and America. Chern did, however, have the opportunity to marry Shih-Ning Cheng, and the couple had their first son, Paul.

By 1943, the war was turning against Japan, and China regained contact with the rest of the world. Chern received an invitation to go to the Institute for Advanced Study at Princeton University (the same institution where Stanislaw Ulam and many other mathematical war refugees would find a home). Chern did important work at the Institute. He proved an important formula called Gauss-Bonnet and wrote about characteristic classes. This work was a development in topology. Topology is often described as a "rubber sheet geometry." If you take a sheet of rubber and draw a figure on it (for example, a triangle), pulling on the edges of the sheet will distort the triangle's shape—its sides will no longer be straight, and its angles will ignore the rules of Euclid and Pythagoras. Nevertheless, topologists can identify characteristics that don't change

> My career is approaching an end and my only question is what to do. The answer is simple. I will continue to play with mathematics.
>
> —Shiing-Shen Chern

when an object is bent out of shape: The triangle, for example, still has an inside and an outside. Holes, too, are preserved—a topological donut may look very weird, but it still has a hole, an inside and outside. Chern contributed to the effort to classify and categorize all the possible ways that things change—and don't change—when various kinds of "transformations" were done on them.

One of Chern's most interesting geometrical discoveries was something called "fiber bundles." Unlike the single kind of space in classical geometry, the bundle represents a "family" of spaces that fan out, each representing a different mathematical solution. What was most surprising, though, is that Chern's fiber bundles turned out to be just the kind of geometry that physicists needed to try to relate together the fundamental forces of the universe—gravity, electromagnetism, and the strong and weak nuclear forces—using equations that describe what are called gauge fields. Physicist Chen Ning Yang told Chern that he "found it amazing that gauge fields are exactly connections on fiber bundles, which the mathematicians developed without reference to the physical world. This is most puzzling, since you mathematicians dreamed up these concepts out of nowhere." But Chern replied "No, no. These concepts were not dreamed up. They were natural and real." Chern believes that when mathematicians and physicists follow their intuition and do enough hard work, they both find "the most beautiful things" that show the deepest connections.

Like Stanislaw Ulam, Chern has had a long and productive working life. He was elected to the United States National Academy of Science in 1961 and he is a foreign member of the British Royal Society. He has been awarded the National Medal of Science and the Wolf Prize. Chern also founded the Berkeley Mathematical Sciences Research Institute in the hills above Berkeley.

Chern did not lose touch with his native land. During the late 1960s and early 1970s, the Cultural Revolution in China led to the torture of many Chinese mathematicians. Starting in 1972, Chern began to visit China regularly, helping to train new Chinese mathematicians at the Nankai University. Chern remembered the creative and productive environment he had experienced at the Institute for Advanced Study at Princeton. In 1985, Chern established the Nankai Mathematical Research Institute, helping Chinese mathematicians to enjoy the same kind of environment.

Shiing-Shen Chern has added much to geometry, the magic map of mathematics. From its solid foundations in Euclid's right angles and triangles, its transformation through projections and curved non-Euclidean spaces and topology's rubber sheets, and onward to fibers and the superstrings of astrophysics, Chern gave a new shape to geometry, and geometry in turn has shaped his life. Now in his eighties, Chern continues to explore the strange worlds of geometry.

Chronology

October 28, 1911	Shiing-Shen Chern born in Kashing, Chekiang Province, China
1926	enrolls in Nankai University
1930	begins graduate study at Tsing Hua University, Peking
1934–1936	attends University of Hamburg
1936–1937	receives doctorate; moves to Paris
1937–1943	war between China and Japan; Chern teaches at temporary university in China
1939	marries Shih-Ning Cheng

1943–1945	does research at Institute for Advanced Study at Princeton; writes paper on "characteristic classes"
1949–1959	teaches at the University of Chicago
1960	moves to the University of California, Berkeley
1972	visits China to train mathematicians
1981	is a principal founder of the Mathematical Sciences Research Institute, Berkeley
1985	founds Nankai Institute for Mathematics in Tianjin, China

Further Reading

Albers, Donald J., and G. L. Alexanderson, eds. *Mathematical People: Profiles and Interviews.* Chicago: Contemporary Books, 1985. This book includes a brief biography of Shiing-Shen Chern.

Paulos, John Allen. *Beyond Numeracy: Ruminations of a Numbers Man.* New York: Vintage Books, 1991. Different kinds of geometry are explored in the chapters on the Pythagorean theorem, non-Euclidean geometry, and topology.

Shing-Tung Yau, ed. *Chern: A Great Geometer of the 20th Century.* Hong Kong: International Press Co., 1992. Includes accounts of Chern's life and work.

*Alan Turing's code-breaking machines helped defeat Hitler in World War II.
Later, he helped develop modern computer designs and prophesied the coming
of artificial intelligence.* (© Photographer, Science Source/Photo Researchers)

Alan Turing

(1912–1954)

Schnell, Schnell!" the German U-boat captain shouted. "Faster, faster!" The men in the engine room struggled to get as much speed as possible out of the engines. That afternoon, the captain had received a secret coded message from U-Boat Command. Turning the wheels on his Enigma cipher machine to the day's code position, he read the message giving the position of a valuable Allied convoy.

The German operators who had sent that message didn't realize it, but their cipher was being broken by British scientists in a secret installation at Bletchley Park. Using mathematical principles developed by Alan Turing in the 1930s, they had designed a cipher-breaking machine that analyzed 25,000 coded characters a second. The British Navy, therefore, knew exactly what orders were being given to German submarines.

It is dawn, and the submarine lies submerged, waiting for its prey. The captain raises his periscope, but not a ship is to be seen. Puzzled, he orders the submarine to surface. But a few minutes later, a lookout shouts "Bomber!" Quickly, the captain orders the U-boat to dive as the plane roars overhead. The hunter had become the hunted. The Germans had lost the war of

> mathematics. Much of the credit for the victory be-
> longed to a brilliant British mathematician and com-
> puter scientist named Alan Turing.

Alan Turing was born in London on June 23, 1912. Because his father was a high official in Britain's colonial government in India, Alan's parents were often away. Alan was raised mainly by relatives until he was school age. He then went as a boarding student to various private schools, finally going to Sherborne School, a "prep," or college preparatory, school.

A British private school was not an easy place for someone who was imaginative and highly individualistic. The school stressed routine, enforced strict discipline, and the older boys "hazed," or systematically harassed, the younger students. Alan survived this abuse and became a good but inconsistent student. Like Srinivasa Ramanujan, his interest in mathematics tended to distract him from his other courses. Alan's mathematics teacher was impressed when he worked out a very advanced number series by himself, but he also complained that the boy "spends a good deal of time apparently in investigations of advanced mathematics to the neglect of elementary work." His chemistry experiments, such as one that featured "very fine colors produced by the ignition of the vapor of super-heated candle grease" also did little to endear him to his teachers. Alan's science reports were " . . . marred by inaccuracy, untidiness, and bad style." Alan often had to make up for poor classwork by getting high marks in the exams held at the end of the semester.

In 1930 Alan won a scholarship and went to King's College of Cambridge University. By then, his mind was ranging through Einstein's physics and the new science of quantum mechanics, and he was starting to tackle the ideas of the most modern mathematics. When Turing had won a mathematics contest back at Sherborne, he had chosen as his prize a copy of a book called *Mathematical Basis of Quantum Mechanics* by John von Neumann. In this book von Neumann showed how the theories being developed by quantum physics were mathematically consistent. He introduced a way of looking at "states" (sets of conditions) and operations (steps needed to get from one state to the next). As with Chern's fiber bundle geometry, the deepest physical realities were turning out to act in ways foreshadowed by "abstract" mathematics.

As the 20th century progressed, mathematics itself was changing in radical ways. Mathematicians such as von Neumann, Bertrand Russell, and Kurt Gödel were trying to do something new: They were using the tools of mathematics to study mathematics itself. David Hilbert asked questions such as "Can you really show that all the rules used by mathematicians are logically consistent?" For example, can you work out all the rules of arithmetic from three basic axioms or assertions: that the number 1 exists, that there is a number after any given number, and that you can make general statements about numbers?

Gödel answered that question by showing that any system of mathematics must contain assertions that can be neither proved nor disproved. To do this, he classified the possible mathematical operations and assigned special "Godel numbers" to them. He then showed that contradictions always emerged. In other words, mathematics was necessarily incomplete.

But Hilbert had also asked "Can you tell whether a given assertion was provable?" If that question could be answered, then mathematicians may not be able to prove a given theorem (such as "every even number is the sum of two prime numbers"), but they would know whether they should keep trying.

This was the problem that Turing now tackled. To do so, he came up with a new approach. Like Babbage a century earlier, Turing asked whether a machine could be built that could be programmed to perform any desired series of mathematical operations. In his paper "On Computable Numbers," published in 1936, Turing designed an imaginary computer that became known as the "Turing Machine." This machine is very simple: You can think of it as a typewriter that has an endless paper tape attached to it. The tape has a succession of little squares that can either have a number 1 in them or nothing at all (which you can think of as "0"). The "typewriter" can move the tape forward or backward a space at a time. It can read whether there is a 1 in that space. The typewriter can be given a table of instructions that say "if you see a 1 in the current space, do this; if you see a 0, do that. The "this" and "that" is a movement instruction (move left, move right, don't move) and a writing instruction (write 1, write 0, don't write anything).

Turing showed how this "universal machine" can be made to perform complex mathematical operations. For example, it could be programmed to find as many digits of pi as one might want. Turing called any number that could be produced by some combination of machine instructions a *computable number*. Turing knew that Cantor had shown that there could be no list containing *all* real numbers, because you could always generate a number not on the list, no matter how long that list. In an analogous way Turing showed that if you try to make a list of "computable numbers," you could show that there would always also be "uncomputable numbers." And that meant that the answer to Hilbert's question was "no, you can't tell for sure whether something can be proved or not."

As it happened, Alonzo Church of Princeton University published a paper at just about the same time. It reached the same conclusion as Turing's paper but used conventional mathematical means rather than Turing's imaginary computer. It would turn out to be the computer ideas, not the pure mathematics, that would be Turing's lasting achievements.

Turing then went to the Institute of Advanced Study at Princeton. Among others, he met John von Neumann, G. H. Hardy, and Albert Einstein, as well as Alonzo Church. Turing had the leisure to work on a variety of ideas. In a letter to his mother, he noted, "You have often asked me about possible applications of various branches of mathematics. I have just discovered a possible application of the kind of thing I am working on at present. It answers the question 'What is the most general kind of code or cipher possible,' and at the same time (rather naturally) enables me to construct a lot of particular and interesting codes."

In 1938, Turing returned to England. In his baggage was a primitive (but working) electro-mechanical computer that he had built. It could multiply two binary numbers (numbers consisting of a series of ones and zeroes). The Turing Machine was starting to become a reality. On September 3, 1939, World War II began in Europe. The next day, Turing joined the British government's Code and Cypher School at Bletchley Park, a mansion in a country town where the railway lines connecting London and Oxford and Cambridge met.

We do not need an infinity of different machines doing different jobs. A single one will suffice. The engineering problem of producing various machines for various jobs is replaced by the office work of "programming" the universal machine to do these jobs.

—Alan Turing

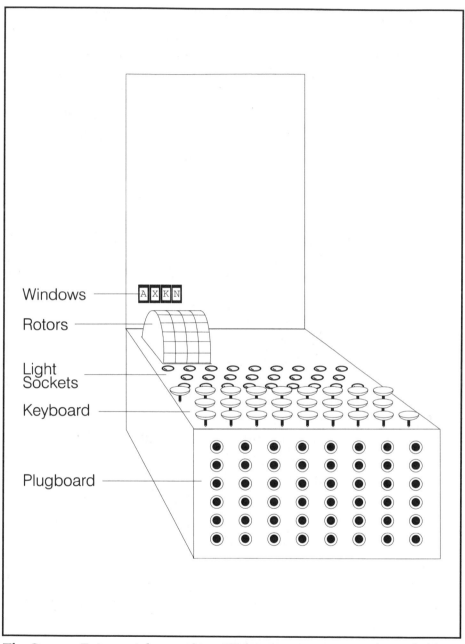

The German Enigma cipher machine. With its moving rotors and switchable plugboard, the device could generate trillions of possible ciphers. It would take blood, sweat, tears—and a computer—to unravel the Enigma. (Courtesy of Katherine Macfarlane)

In its simplest form a cipher is a system where a message (called *plain text*) is turned into a coded message (or *cipher text*) by substituting a different letter for each letter in the message. For example, if each letter were replaced with the next letter in the alphabet, the word *war* would be encoded as *xbs*. A simple cipher like this would be easy to guess, so in practice ciphering systems used more complicated rules or made a repeated series of substitutions. The cipher machine used by the Germans, called Enigma, created a very complex mechanical cipher. To send a message, the operator first set three (later four) wheels called rotors so that the letters for that day's code showed in the window. The operator also made specified connections in a "plug board" on the front of the machine. When the operator typed a letter of the plain text, a light would light up to show the corresponding letter of cipher text. As the rotors moved, they created a continuously changing cipher. Because of the use of three rotors, the movable rings used to set the rotors, and the plug board, the Enigma machine had trillions of possible settings. This led the Germans to believe that their code system was unbreakable.

In 1932, however, French agents had been able to obtain an instruction manual for Enigma machine operators. The Polish Secret Service was given a copy, and the Poles put three mathematicians to work figuring out from the instructions how the Enigma rotors were wired. Further, the instructions gave all the information needed to encode two months worth of messages *except* the rotor positions. Because the rotor settings had to be sent by each Engima operator before sending the message, code-breakers were able to decode the rotor settings (the fact that they were always repeated twice made it easier to figure them out). Until 1938, therefore, the Poles, French, and other likely enemies of Germany had the ability to break German Enigma codes.

In 1938, the Germans introduced a more complicated system that was harder to decode. But again, cryptanalysts (cipher-breakers) were able to take advantage of certain patterns of repeated letters to break the ciphers. The problem was that a given pattern had to be matched against thousands of possible combinations. The Poles solved this problem by essentially building copies of the Enigma machine and wiring them together so that they would step through the rotor positions and look for key patterns. Because the machine made a ticking sound while it was running, it was nicknamed the "Bombe."

But at the very end of 1938, the Germans increased the number of rotors that could be chosen by an Enigma operator from three to five (of which three could be used in the machine at any one time). There were now not six but 60 ($5 \times 4 \times 3$) possible combinations of rotors. Decoding them would require a "Bombe" with 60 machines—too many to be practicable.

When the war broke out in 1939 and the British were given the results of the Polish research, they were dismayed. Any rigid mechanical decoding system could be made obsolete simply by the Germans introducing new rotors. They needed a more general, programmable machine that could scan for patterns in the Enigma messages. They had to take advantage of the fact that each of the millions of Enigma settings had its own internal consistency. The fact that certain letters were encoded as certain other letters meant that certain other possible letter matchings could not be true.

Fortunately Turing had worked out the theory for just such a machine in his "Computable Numbers" paper. And asking whether a number was "computable" was somewhat like asking whether a given cipher message *could* match a given plain text, allowing for possible plugboard swappings. Using a technique called traffic analysis and looking for patterns, the cipher-breakers could use "probable words" and construct a machine that would use Turing's methods to test them against the possibilities.

Even aided by the new machines, the actual cipher-breaking process would require many months to get up to speed. But by mid-1941, the British were decoding German naval messages almost as fast as their recipients were reading them.

But in February 1942, the Germans redesigned their Enigma machines by attaching a fourth rotor to the end. Since this rotor had 26 possible settings, there were now 26 times as many possibilities for the "Bombes" to check. And so the contest between the German Enigma and the British code-breakers would continue. The Germans would add complications; Turing and the other British experts would respond by coming up with ways to make better guesses, and with machines that could check patterns from paper tape and, eventually, store some of them electronically. In 1943, Turing helped build COLOSSUS, an early computer that could do more than just break codes.

When the war ended, Turing, like von Neumann in the United States, was thinking in terms of general-purpose computers. (On a wartime visit to America, Turing had met Claude Shannon of Bell Laboratories, whose work on information theory and Boolean-coded circuitry meshed well with Turing's knowledge of computation theory.)

The possibilities for computing machines in the postwar world were exciting, but the challenges were equally great. Would the switching that would transmit the binary numbers be done with slower, more reliable electric relays, or with the much faster but less reliable electronic vacuum tubes? How could information be stored "in memory" for later use? And how could programs be written in such a way that they broke complex mathematical problems down into a sequence of simple steps and decision branches that could be performed by the computer? Turing, who worked on the design of a machine called the Pilot ACE, made a number of contributions to computer design and programming, including a way to have a computer change its own stored program instructions according to the data it was working with.

The most interesting work of Turing's later life involved what we call today artificial intelligence. Turing had a lifelong interest in chess and began to sketch out strategies for a computerized chess player. The main problem was figuring out rules that the machine could use to determine the best move in a given position—something that a good human player does through a mixture of recognizing patterns and using intuition.

Philosophers were beginning to ask whether a computer might someday be able to think in the sense that human beings think. This, of course, led to endless discussions about what was meant by "thought" and how the human brain actually works. But Turing took a typically original approach in a paper called "Computing Machinery and Intelligence" that he wrote in 1950. He imagined a person sitting at a teletype machine. The person could type messages on the keyboard, and in turn someone

> The original question, "Can machines think?" I believe to be too meaningless to deserve discussion. Nevertheless at the end of the century the use of words and general educated opinion will have altered so much that one will be able to speak of machines thinking without expecting to be contradicted.
>
> —Alan Turing

or something could type replies from the other end of the line. The person's job was to determine whether the other end of the phone line had a person—or a computer. Turing said that "I believe that in about fifty years' time it will be possible to program computers . . . to make them play the imitation game so well that an average interrogator will not have more than a 70 per cent chance of making the right identification after five minutes of questioning." Ever since, artificial intelligence researchers have considered whether some new computer program might pass the "Turing Test."

Like the lives of several other mathematicians in this book, Alan Turing's life was tragically cut short. The master code-breaker had a secret of his own: He was a homosexual. In Britain in the 1950s, the harsh laws against gay sex offered a choice of prison or treatment by hormone injections. Near the end of 1951, an unwise affair led to Turing's arrest, conviction, and sentence of medical treatment. Turing seemed to cope well with his misfortune, but on June 7, 1954, he killed himself with cyanide. The authorities ruled it a suicide, but Turing's mother believed that it might have been a careless accident.

Fifty years after Turing's pioneering computer work, computer hardware has changed beyond what anyone could have imagined then. The computers on our desktops are thousands of times more powerful than the room-filling machines of the early 1950s. A computer the size of a pocket calculator can now play chess better than anyone but an expert. There are programs that can carry on conversations that can under certain circumstances pass the Turing Test. But no computer has yet shown the general, wide-ranging intelligence that human beings possess.

Chronology

June 23, 1912	Alan Turing born in London
1930	enters King's College, Cambridge University
1936	writes prize-winning paper "On Computable Numbers"
1937–1938	studies at Princeton University; earns doctorate
September 1939	World War II begins
1939	begins to work on German cipher 5 at Bletchley Park
December 1943	Prototype COLOSSUS computer begins operation
1951	Turing elected fellow of British Royal Society
June 7, 1954	Alan Turing dies

Further Reading

Ashhurst, F. Gareth. *Pioneers of Computing*. London: Frederick Muller, 1983. Has a chapter that briefly summarizes Turing's life and work.

Hodges, Andrew. *Alan Turing: The Enigma*. New York: Simon & Schuster, 1983. Full-length biography of Alan Turing. Includes detailed discussion of his work and personal life.

Lewin, Ronald. *Ultra Goes to War : The First Account of World War II's Greatest Secret Based on Official Documents*. New York: McGraw-Hill, 1978. This book gives details on how the "Ultra" team broke German wartime ciphers, and on how their achievement helped the Allied war effort.

McCorduck, Pamela. *Machines Who Think: A Personal Inquiry into the History and Prospects of Artificial Intelligence*. San Francisco: W. H. Freeman, 1979. This is a fascinating and readable account of how artificial intelligence research developed following the work of Alan Turing, John von Neumann, and other pioneers.

Julia Bowman Robinson. One of the first great American women mathematicians, Robinson found the solution to one of the great unsolved problems of mathematics—with the help of a young Russian. (Reprinted by permission of the American Mathematical Society)

Julia Bowman Robinson

(1919–1985)

$\mathbf{M}$athematics is like a conversation carried on across the ages. Sometimes it might be generations before a question one mathematician asks is answered by another.

Around 1900, David Hilbert made a list of problems that mathematicians had not solved. About 70 years later an American woman mathematician, Julia Bowman Robinson, solved one of these problems. Hilbert, who had tried to help Sofia Kovalevskaia get a job, would probably have been pleased that a woman mathematician had come up with the solution.

Julia Bowman was born on December 8, 1919, in St. Louis, Missouri. Her mother died when she was only two years old, and Julia and her sister Constance went to live with their grandmother in Phoenix, Arizona. Their father soon remarried and the newly completed family continued to live in Arizona for several years.

Julia was considered to be a "slow" child. She had trouble talking, and her older sister Constance did most of her talking for her. But Julia overcame her problems. She had a stubbornness that she would later say was largely responsible for her success in mathematics.

Julia felt that she had "always had a basic liking for the natural numbers. To me they are the one real thing. We can conceive of a chemistry that is different from ours, or a biology, but we cannot conceive of a different mathematics of numbers. What is proved about numbers will be a fact in any universe."*

Julia's mind first really focused on mathematics after she had been sick for a year with scarlet fever. The disease weakened her heart, and she had to stay in bed. When she was well enough, the family got her a tutor who quickly brought her through the courses for the fifth, sixth, seventh, and eighth grades. One day the tutor pointed out to Julia that if one tried to work out the square root of two, the result was a decimal number that never ended and never repeated. Julia wanted to see for herself, and spent a whole afternoon generating digits from this square root.

In 1932, Julia entered the ninth grade at a regular junior high school. She did well in math there, and then she took courses in plane geometry, algebra, advanced algebra, trigonometry, and solid geometry. After that geometry course (which was required) Julia found that she was the only girl still taking mathematics. She was also the only girl in physics class. Despite her shyness, Julia found other interests besides mathematics—including art and baseball (where she became fascinated by the sport's many statistics).

Following high school, Julia Bowman made a decision that was rather surprising at that time. In the 1930s, most American women did not go to college. Most women who did go to college took courses that prepared them for teaching elementary or high school. Bowman's parents

---

*This and other quotations by Julia Bowman were actually written by her sister Constance Reid, who wrote about Julia's life as though it were an autobiography by Julia in the first person.

thought that a teaching credential would help her earn a living until, as her father said, "You can marry a college professor."

Bowman went to what is now San Diego State University, where her sister was already studying. Julia Bowman majored in mathematics. Besides studying calculus, she encountered a book by E. T. Bell called *Men of Mathematics*. This book did two things: It introduced her to many interesting problems in number theory, and it gave her a picture of life as a mathematician. Bowman eventually decided that rather than continuing to work for a teaching credential (which didn't seem to guarantee a job, anyway), she would go where she could learn to be a mathematician.

Bowman went to the University of California at Berkeley. Unlike her time at high school and junior college, Bowman found that there were many other students at Berkeley who shared her enthusiasm for mathematics. When socializing with the faculty, she met Raphael M. Robinson. Julia and Raphael were soon taking walks where they discussed exciting new developments in mathematics. One such development was Gödel's symbolic proof that mathematics was incomplete. What impressed her most was that mathematical symbols could be used to study not just rules about numbers but rules about mathematics itself.

Bowman's mother became anxious that she find a "real" job, but

I was especially excited by some of the theorems of number theory, and I used to recount these to Constance at night after we went to bed. She soon found that if she wasn't ready to go to sleep she could keep me awake by asking questions about mathematics.

—Julia Bowman

Raphael convinced her to stay on at Berkeley and become a teaching assistant. In late 1941, just a few weeks before the Japanese attack on Pearl Harbor, Julia and Raphael were married.

Julia believed that Raphael's support and encouragement had been a key factor in her staying with her decision to become a mathematician. Unfortunately, there was a rule that a husband and wife could not teach in the same university department. (This rule was designed to prevent nepotism, or the giving of unfair advantages to one's relatives. A practical effect of this policy, however, was that it tended to prevent married women from getting jobs in science or mathematics, since they often had husbands who worked in the same field.)

Julia was not too upset with this interruption in her career, because she wanted to have children. Unfortunately, the damage to her heart she had suffered as a child turned out to make childbearing too dangerous. Julia was very disappointed, but her husband encouraged her to turn her attention back to mathematics.

In 1942, Julia Robinson heard a lecture on number theory by Alfred Tarski, a Polish mathematician who had been stranded in America by the outbreak of World War II. Tarski brought up a fundamental question about number theory: Can addition be defined in terms of succession (the fact that numbers followed one another) and multiplication? Robinson played around with the problem and came up with a complicated and quite original definition. Tarski was very impressed with her work. He became Robinson's thesis advisor. In her thesis, Robinson looked at how integers could be defined in relation to multiplication, addition, and the idea of rational numbers (rational numbers are numbers that can be expressed as fractions, such as $^4/_1$ or $^1/_3$). In essence, Robinson extended work that had been done on whole numbers (integers) to the field of all rational numbers.

In 1948, Robinson got her Ph.D. She then became interested in a problem that had been posed near the beginning of the century by David Hilbert. Hilbert had made a list of what were at the time the most important unsolved problems in mathematics. The 10th problem on Hilbert's list had to do with whether one could determine whether a particular kind of equation could be solved.

The roots of this problem went back to Pierre de Fermat, a mathematician who had lived in the 17th century. The question was this: Are there solutions for equations of the form $X^n + Y^n = Z^n$, where n represents a power of three (a cube) or higher? There were solutions where n was 2: For example, $3^2 + 4^2 = 5^2$. But mathematicians had found no solutions where the sum of two cubes equaled a third cube. Fermat wrote a note in one of his books that read "I have discovered a marvelous proof . . . but this margin is too small to hold it." Ever since, mathematicians had tried to find the elusive proof.

Hilbert's problem generalized Fermat's theorem to apply to something called diophantine equations. These equations, discussed by Diophantus in the third century, consist of several variables raised to various powers and multiplied by whole numbers. For example, $X^2 - 94Y^2 = 1$ is a diophantine equation. Not all diophantine equations have solutions that are whole numbers, and it is not easy to tell which ones can be solved. (The example equation does have a solution: X = 2,143,295 and Y= 221,064. This is clearly a job for a fast computer!)

Robinson "sneaked up" on this problem by working on various problems that if solved would become steps toward a complete solution. For example, she considered whether every power of 2 could be expressed as the solution of a diophantine equation. Although she was unable to solve this problem, she made progress on related problems in a paper with the title "Existential Definability in Arithmetic."

In the early 1950s, Robinson's research took several detours. First, she worked with the RAND corporation and became interested in finding a strategy for "zero sum games." A zero sum game is a situation where there are two players. The first player makes a "random" move. The second player makes the move that best counters the first move. The first player then finds a move that is the average of the first two moves, the second player averages the second and third moves, and so on. Robinson showed that if each player pursues a strategy that is the average of the values of the last two moves, the moves "converge" toward a solution of the game.

Robinson also was persuaded to spend a year doing work on the mathematics of hydrodynamics (the study of fluids). She worked hard but couldn't accomplish anything. After that year, she found she had an interest in politics and helped with several political campaigns.

Robinson had not forgotten Hilbert's Tenth Problem, however. In 1961, she co-authored a paper with Martin Davis and Hilary Putnam. It suggested a possible approach to solving Hilbert's problem by looking at exponentiation (numbers increasing by a power) and polynomials

All this attention, has been gratifying but also embarassing. What I really am is a mathematician. Rather than being remembered as the first woman this or that, I would prefer to be remembered as a mathematician should, simply for the theorems I have proved and the problems I have solved.

—Julia Bowman Robinson

(equations that use both multipliers and powers, such as $ax^2 + 5x - 5 = 0$). Robinson suggested that there were diophantine equations that increased faster than polynomials but slower than exponentials.

That same year, Robinson's weak heart broke down, and she had to have surgery to clear one of its valves. She responded in typical fashion: As soon as she was up and around, she bought a bicycle and began to take long rides. She also kept working on the Hilbert problem, though she became discouraged when she seemed to hit a dead end.

On February 15, 1970, Martin Davis called her with news from Moscow. A Russian mathematician, only 22 years old, had supplied the missing piece to the Hilbert puzzle. The "Robinson hypothesis" turned out to be correct. The answer to Hilbert was that there was no way to prove that a given diophantine equation had a whole-number solution. Delighted, Robinson wrote to the young Russian mathematician ". . . now I know it is true, it is beautiful, it is wonderful. If you really are 22, I am especially pleased to think that when I first made the conjecture you were a baby and I just had to wait for you to grow up."

The solution to the Hilbert problem brought attention and awards to Robinson. In 1975, she became the first woman mathematician to be elected to the National Academy of Sciences. In 1982, she was nominated for the presidency of the American Mathematical Society. Despite the added burden on her health, Robinson felt she had to accept the honor on behalf of women, whom she had always encouraged and helped in their mathematical careers.

In August 1984, Robinson learned that she had leukemia. She died on July 30, 1985, at the age of 65.

Chronology

December 8, 1919	Julia Robinson born in St. Louis, Missouri
1930	recovering from illness, Robinson becomes interested in mathematics
1937	enters state college in San Diego
1939	enters University of California at Berkeley
1941	marries Raphael Robinson
1948	writes thesis on number theory for doctorate at Berkeley
1961	contributes to paper on Hilbert's Tenth Problem
1970	a Russian mathematician completes the solution to Hilbert's problem
1975	Robinson becomes first woman mathematician to be elected to National Academy of Sciences
1982	becomes president of American Mathematical Society
July 30, 1985	Julia Bowman Robinson dies

Further Reading

Albers, Donald J., Gerald L.Alexanderson, and Constance Reid, eds. *More Mathematical People.* Has an "autobiography" of Julia Bowman Robinson written by her sister Constance Reid, a noted popular writer on mathematics.

Dunham, William. *The Mathematical Universe*. New York: John Wiley & Sons, 1994. Chapter titled "Where Are the Women?" provides background on the growing presence of women in modern mathematics.

Paulos, John Allen. *Beyond Numeracy*. New York: Vintage Books, 1992. Has many short chapters on interesting mathematical problems. See "Fermat's Last Theorem" for more on Fermat and on the general problem posed by David Hilbert.

Benoit Mandelbrot unlocked a dazzling world of fractals. Fractals, with their endless patterns within patterns, are an aspect of chaos—the new science that finds order in seeming randomness. (Reprinted from *I Have a Photographic Memory,* by Paul R. Halmos, by permission of the American Mathematical Society)

Benoit Mandelbrot

(1 9 2 4 –)

Y̶ou call up a screen on your personal computer and enter some data. A program called FRACTINT plugs your data into an equation and uses the equation to plot thousands of points of colored light on the screen. As you watch, rainbow swirls more intricate than coral reefs begin to surround a lake of blue. You take your mouse, point and click at an interesting-looking swirl, and the computer zooms into it like a microscope. Inside the swirl are other swirls surrounding another lake. Time after time, you plunge into a tiny corner of the picture, only to see the next universe in all its complexity and glory. Like an onion with endless layers, the patterns unfold.

You are seeing a new kind of mathematics called fractal geometry. In discovering this new geometry with its endless layers of unique patterns, Benoit Mandelbrot found the order hidden inside the seeming chaos of nature.

Benoit Mandelbrot was born in Warsaw, Poland, on November 20, 1924. His family was Jewish and had originally come from Lithuania. They were well-educated, but Benoit's father had to work as a clothing manufacturer.

In 1936, when Benoit was 12 and Hitler was beginning to threaten Europe, the family moved to Paris. Benoit's uncle

Szolem Mandelbroit taught mathematics as a university professor, and Benoit grew up meeting mathematicians and hearing mathematical talk. Like Shiing-Shen Chern, Benoit became especially interested in geometry. His uncle, who worked in advanced analysis (calculus), did not approve of this interest. He shared the opinon of many mathematicians of the time that geometry had reached a dead end and was suitable only for beginning students.

In 1940, the Germans occupied France. The Mandelbrot family had to move frequently to avoid the Nazis. It was impossible for young Benoit to have regular schooling. "For awhile, I was moving around with a younger brother, toting around a few obsolete books and learning things my way, guessing a number of things myself, doing nothing in any rational or even half-reasonable way, and acquiring a great deal of independence and self-confidence."

When Paris was liberated in 1944, Benoit took the examinations for entry into French universities. Although he had never studied advanced algebra or calculus, Benoit found that his familiarity and fondness for geometry helped him "translate" problems in other kinds of mathematics into familiar forms. Shapes seemed to be Benoit's natural friends in the way that Ramanujan had considered every natural number to be a personal friend.

In 1945, Benoit's uncle returned from the United States, where he had stayed during the war. They argued about Benoit's future career. Szolem

Faced with some complicated integral, I instantly related it to a familiar shape … I knew an army of shapes that I'd encountered once in some book or some problem, and remembered forever, with their properties and their peculiarities.

—Benoit Mandelbrot

supported a mathematical movement called Bourbaki, which stressed a style of mathematical analysis that was formal, strict, and elegant. Benoit resisted his uncle's suggestions. Perhaps because his youth had been spent in a world of constant change, Benoit instinctively sought a field that would have rough edges and texture—a world of changing geometric shapes.

At the Polytechnique School of Paris, Mandebrot found a mathematician who shared this spirit of adventure: Paul Lévy. Lévy had become an expert in probability theory and had also studied physical phenomena that involved probability, such as Brownian motion, the jittery random way that small particles move in response to heat energy. Lévy hepled Mandelbrot learn to look for mathematical phenomena in nature rather than only in the neat, tidy abstractions favored by many established mathematicians.

In 1952 Mandelbrot got his Ph.D. from the University of Paris. His doctoral thesis brought together ideas from thermodynamics (the part of physics that deals with the way heat does work in physical systems), the cybernetics (computer theory) of Norbert Wiener, and the game theory of John von Neumann. Mandelbrot later said that the thesis was poorly written and badly organized, but it did reflect his continuing attempt to bring together mathematics and the physical world in new ways.

In 1953–1954 Mandelbrot, like many of the "mathematical refugees" in this book, went to the Institute for Advanced Studies at Princeton. He continued to explore many different fields of mathematics. In 1955 he returned to France and married Aliette Kagan.

The work that would bring together all of Mandelbrot's interests began in 1958, when he accepted an open-ended position at the research department at International Business Machines (IBM). IBM was becoming the leader of the computer industry, and it, like Bell Telephone, had a policy of giving selected "cutting edge" scientists some money and a laboratory and letting them pursue their interests. Although the work they funded often had no direct connection with computers or telephones, such programs often resulted in important technical advances.

In 1960, Mandelbrot began to notice unusual patterns in seemingly random data. Although he had no background in economics, Mandelbrot realized that economics is a good source of "random" data. For example, the price of a commodity (such as cotton) usually moves in two manners. One kind of move has some reasonable cause, such as bad weather reducing the amount of the product available. The other kind of movement seems to be erratic or random—the prices "jiggle" up and down by small amounts from hour to hour or day to day.

Economists assumed that if the random price fluctuations were plotted on a graph, they would form the well-known "bell curve" pattern. (When a class is "graded on a curve" there are only a few As and Fs, more Bs and Ds, and the largest group of grades are Cs. The curve "bulges" in the middle at C and tapers off as you move toward the F or A ends.) In other words, he expected that most prices would hover near the average value.

Mandelbrot had been invited by Hendrick Houthakker, a Harvard economics professor, to give a talk to his students. When Mandelbrot arrived at Houthakker's office, the graph he saw on the blackboard there looked strangely familiar. Mandelbrot had been graphing the distribution of incomes in a group of people. He had been finding that the incomes didn't fall neatly into a bell curve. They tended to make a longer, flatter curve, with "clumps" of incomes scattered throughout. Houthakker's graph looked very similar— although it turned out to represent not incomes, but cotton prices.

Mandelbrot later recalled that he "had identified a new phenomenon present in many aspects of nature, but all the examples were peripheral in their fields, and the phenomenon itself had eluded definition. The usual term now is the Greek *chaos,* but I had been using the weaker-sounding Latin term *erratic behavior* at the time."

The "erratic behavior" that had showed up in incomes and cotton prices had also appeared in physics in the jittery motion of small dust particles or gas molecules. In geometry, it showed up in patterns that were made up of tiny clumps that were distributed seemingly randomly. The patterns lacked the neatness of the straight lines and smooth curves of Euclidean geometry, but the patterns were "self-similar," that is, if you magnified the pattern, each part looked like a miniature copy of the whole. This could be done indefinitely, moving to a smaller and smaller scale. Mandelbrot used the word *fractal* (meaning fractured or broken up) to describe these geometric patterns.

Mandelbrot often began his lectures on fractal geometry by asking "How long is the coastline of Britain?" This question is deceptively simple. If you look at a map of Britain in an atlas and place a ruler along the coast to form a series of straight lines, you might draw 8 such lines representing 200 miles each—for a total length of 1,600 miles. But if you use shorter lines of 25 miles each that

> Science would be ruined if (like sports) it were to put competition above everything else, and if it were to clarify the rules of competition by withdrawing entirely into narrowly defined specialties. The rare scholars who are wanderers-by-choice are essential to the intellectual welfare of the settled disciplines.
>
> —Benoit Mandelbrot

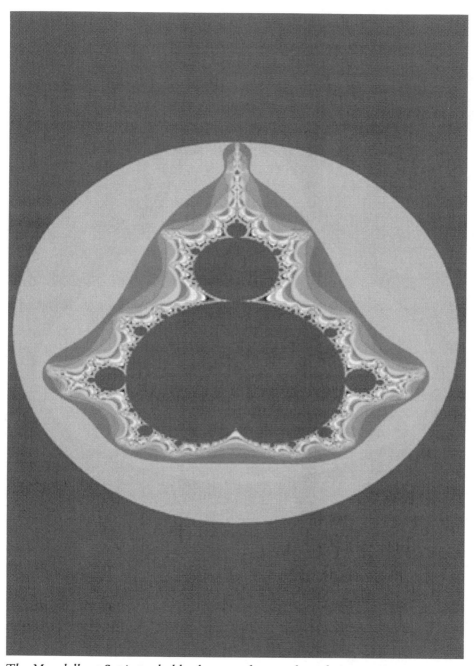

The Mandelbrot Set is probably the most famous fractal. As you zoom into any part, you find the structure is repeated in miniature. (Courtesy of The Waite Group)

fit the zigs and zags of the coastline more accurately, you might get 102 lines for a total length of 2,550 miles. If you then get local maps and start measuring the coastline in each region, the total length will increase as the measurements get smaller and more precise. Eventually, you might walk to the beach and measure the edge of the beach among the boulders and sand castles. The more you "zoom in" on it, the more detail you see. The coastline is a fractal: Instead of having just one dimension (as a line on a map), it has a "fractional" dimension of about 1.2. Put another way, it "stuffs" many extra zigs and zags into its single dimension of space.

Since the 1960s, many different types of fractals have been discovered. Each has an equation that generates a series of complex numbers ("complex" here doesn't mean "complicated"; it means extended to include "imaginary" numbers such as the square root of –1. Imaginary numbers were developed in order to make the system of mathematics consistent and complete). When Mandelbrot started generating fractals, he had to use IBM mainframe computers that were fed with punch cards. Today, a desktop PC can generate many kinds of fractal images and show them on the screen in full color. Perhaps the most famous fractal image is called the Mandelbrot set, in honor of its discoverer.

Many scientists were slow to realize and accept the general application of Mandelbrot's ideas. After all, the existing statistical methods worked pretty well for most applications, and resulted in neat and comprehensible charts and graphs. Fractals and chaos theory involved strange shapes, randomness, and uncertainty—and a new kind of mathematics. People trained in classical geometry sometimes lacked Mandelbrot's ability to use his intuition to make sense of strange-yet-familiar shapes.

By the 1970s, Mandelbrot and other researchers had extended their theories of fractal geometry and chaotic behavior into many aspects of nature. Mandelbrot's two popular books, *Fractals: Form, Chance, and Dimension* (1977) and *The Fractal Geometry of Nature* (1982) include many examples of fractals such as snowflakes, mountains, and coastlines. The science of chaos has been applied to weather forecasting, the distribution of galaxies in the universe, transmission of signals on phone lines, and ways to compress pictures so they can be stored more efficiently in a computer. Even in biology, fractals have been shown to be related to such things as the structure of a fern and the branching of the human circulatory system. As people working in different fields of science began to acknowledge the importance of Mandelbrot's work, he was awarded many prizes in fields as diverse as mathematics, physics, engineering, and even medicine. He continues to explore the applications of fractals and chaos theory today.

Chronology

November 20, 1924	Benoit Mandelbrot born in Warsaw, Poland
1936	growth of Nazi power leads Mandelbrot family to move to France
1940–1943	Mandelbrot family become war refugees
1944	Allies liberate France; Mandelbrot begins university education
1952	gets doctorate in mathematics at University of Paris
1953–1954	studies at Institute for Advanced Study at Princeton
1958	begins career at IBM research center
1960–1962	studies chaotic data in economics
1975	coins the term "fractal"
1986–1994	wins numerous scientific awards

Further Reading

Albers, Donald J. and G. L. Alexanderson, eds. *Mathematical People: Profiles and Interviews.* Chicago: Contemporary Books, 1985. Has a chapter with background and an interview with Benoit Mandelbrot.

Gleick, James. *Chaos: Making a New Science.* New York: Penguin Books, 1987. Has a chapter about Mandelbrot's work on fractals, placing it in the larger setting of chaos theory, the branch of mathematics that finds surprising patterns within apparently random phenomena.

Mandelbrot, Benoit. *Fractals: Form, Chance, and Dimension.* San Francisco: W. H. Freeman, 1977. Mandelbrot's book on fractals for the general reader, includes illustrations and applications of fractals to many branches of science.

Wegner, Tim and Bert Tyler. *Fractal Creations.* 2nd ed. Corte Madera, California: Waite Group Press, 1993. Introduces fractal theory, illustrates dozens of different "families" of fractals, and provides software you can use to design your own fractals.

John H. Conway loves to invent new games and puzzles. His Game of Life showed how simple rules could create complex patterns that behave in lifelike ways. (Carol Baxter/Mathematical Association of America)

John H. Conway

(1937–)

If you could visit the common room of the mathematics department at the University of Cambridge in the late 1960s, you might well wonder if everyone has gone crazy. Tables and floors are covered with ruled graph paper. Bunches of shells, counters, coins, and Go stones are arranged in intricate patterns on hundreds of squares. A student stares at a particular pattern and then, in a sudden burst of activity, moves its pieces to form a different pattern. Other students are arguing earnestly about things called blinkers, honey farms, and glider guns. What is going on?

The students were playing something called the Game of Life. This was no ordinary game. Its rules were much simpler than those of chess. The game had no winners or losers. Yet its inventor, mathematician John Horton Conway, would use it to show how the most complex things, perhaps even living creatures, might arise from a set of simple rules.

John Horton Conway* was born on December 26, 1937, in Liverpool, England. John's father was a laboratory assistant at the Liverpool Institute for Boys, and John was thus

---

*John Horton Conway should not be confused with another mathematician, John B. Conway.

exposed to science and mathematics from an early age. John quickly showed a talent for doing complex calculations in his head. His mother later claimed that John was reciting powers of 2 (2, 4, 8, 16, 32, and so on) when he was only four years old.

Conway did well in all his school classes. He received his B.A. at the University of Cambridge in 1959; by 1962 he had his doctorate and a reputation for being brilliant but rather "quirky." In 1969, Conway, by then married and with four daughters, was seeking to establish a firm place for himself in the world of mathematics. "I knew that I was a good mathematician, but the world didn't," Conway says.

Conway then discovered a geometrical object that existed in an imaginary 24-dimensional space. Mathematicians who heard about it hoped that Conway's discovery would lead to an advance in group theory and a better understanding of symmetry (the ways that objects have parts that "mirror" each other along certain dimensions). With a small income and four children to raise, Conway at first thought it would be years before he could find the time needed for turning his discovery into a complete theory. But when he started his first work session, he emerged $12^1/_2$ hours later with the theory of his new object all worked out. The result became known as a Conway group, and it suddenly made him a world-class mathematician.

But Conway would become most famous for his mathematical puzzles

Dr. Ronald I. Graham of Bell Laboratories describes Conway as:

"One of the most original mathematicians. He's definitely world class, yet he has this kind of childlike enthusiasm. He's confident enough to work on any crazy thing he wants to."

and games. He seemed to generate an endless supply of amusements that also served the purpose of making mathematical concepts graspable—and fun. Conway folded bits of paper into elaborate shapes and challenged bystanders to figure them out. He created games involving geometry or topology. One game, which Conway co-invented with Michael Stewart Patterson, was called Sprouts. The rules were simple: The game starts with a piece of paper with two spots marked on it. A player can join any two spots (or join a spot to itself) with a curve, provided that the curve doesn't cross any curve already drawn. The player then puts a spot somewhere on the new curve. Play ends when one player can't draw a curve without crossing another curve or crossing a spot that is already connected to three curves.

Another game, Philosopher's Football, or "phutball," uses a Go board and stones. A black stone placed at the center of the board represents the "ball." Players take turns either placing a white stone at any intersection on the board (to block opponent's possible moves) or jumping the ball over one or more stones in a way similar to jumping in checkers. The winner is the player who can jump the ball over the opponent's edge of the board (the goal line).

But Conway's most famous game grew out of his interest in automata. During the 1950s, John von Neumann had worked with the idea that a machine could be designed that could grow, reproduce, and interact with its environment. If so, von Neumann argued, one might have to call the machine "alive."

Von Neumann decided it would not be possible to build a real, functioning machine of this type with the available technology. Instead, he sketched out a kind of model showing the logic that a machine might use to carry out its life processes. As he worked on it, the design grew more and more complicated. It became difficult to keep track of the activities of the machine's thousands of separate parts.

Meanwhile, Stanislaw Ulam had been doing pioneering work in computer simulations. The computer made it possible to test logical systems that were too complex for human calculators to keep up with. Ulam programmed sets of rules that the computer would use to draw patterns on a grid of squares. The patterns often turned out to be surprisingly complex and beautiful (one set of rules generated a delicate, coral-like growth from a single square).

Ulam worked with von Neumann to translate his "living machine" concepts into a set of rules that could be used to manipulate patterns on the computer. Ulam and von Neumann hoped that they could at least simulate a "living machine" in the computer, leaving the actual construction of the machine to a future generation.

"What turned me on was this mysterious relationship between things. There is this wonderful world of logic and connections that is very difficult to see. I can see trees and cats and people, but there's this other world and it's very, very powerful."

—John H. Conway

Ulam put von Neumann's machine into a "world" that consisted of an endless grid of squares that he called "cells." The cells would behave according to a set of rules that would determine their new state according to the conditions of their surroundings. For example, a cell that was surrounded by enough "food" cells might change from one state where the cell is surviving but not growing, to another state where one of its neighbors is added to the growing "organism."

Von Neumann's final design for his "living" automaton was very complex. There were 200,000 cells that, like the cells in the human body, had different specialties (such as copying information, growing, or reproducing). Cells could have any one of 29 possible states—represented by different colors. Because of its use of many individual cells governed by automatic rules, the simulated organism became known as a "cellular automaton."

Von Neumann's health failed before he could demonstrate a computer simulation of his "living" automaton. Ulam went on to other projects. The field of cellular automation faded away from the attention of mathematicians until around 1968, when Conway began thinking about the subject.

Von Neumann's and Ulam's automaton was very complex and used many possible states. Conway decided to see what could be done with a logical world where the cells can have only two states, which can be called "on" and "off" or "living" and "dead." Each cell would evaluate its surrounding cells, and respond according to a set of simple rules. As a result, the cell would live or die. As the pattern was stepped through many "generations," the patterns would grow, die, or shift around on the grid of squares.

Conway tried several different kinds of rules for life and death, seeking the rules that would result in the most interesting patterns. His final rules are as follows:

- Start with a grid of cells (like a piece of graph paper).
- Mark certain cells as being "on" or "alive." You can mark these cells by putting objects (such as coins or Go stones) in them.
- Now look at each cell on the grid.
- Check the eight cells that surround that cell.
- Count the number of surrounding cells that are "alive."
- If exactly two neighbors are alive, the state of the current cell does not change. (That is, if it's alive, it stays alive. If it's dead, it stays dead.) If there are three neighbors alive, however, the cell will be alive, even if it is currently dead. Finally, if the number of living neighbors is neither 2 nor 3, the cell will be dead, even

if it is currently alive. The process of checking the neighbors of every cell on the grid is called a "generation."

Conway and his students found that these simple rules produced a startling variety of patterns, depending on what kind of pattern you started the game with. A row of three living cells, which Conway called a "blinker," would alternate between vertical and horizontal. An L-shaped pattern of three cells turned into a four-cell block—and after that, stayed the same forever. Some patterns, such as a T-shaped pattern of four cells, took on a bewildering variety of forms as the generations passed.

Conway called his pattern generator the "Game of Life," and it was first publicized in two articles in *Scientific American* magazine in 1970 and 1971. Soon people were writing letters that included their own newly discovered Life patterns. As the 1970s moved on, more and more students and hobbyists were getting access to computers. The Game of Life could be easily translated into a computer program that could plot the grid cells on the computer screen or print them out on paper. By 1974, *Time* magazine was noting that "millions of dollars in valuable computer time may already have been wasted by the game's growing horde of fanatics."

But Life was not just fun and games. Serious-minded mathematicians began to ask intriguing questions about the Life universe. Was there a Life pattern that would grow bigger and bigger without ever stopping? Or does every pattern eventually either die out or turn into a stable configuration (where the patterns either stopped moving or, like the "blinker," repeated the same sequence of forms over and over)?

One day one of Conway's colleagues, Richard Guy, pointed at a Life board and said in surprise, "Oh, look. My bit's walking." This object, consisting of five cells, went

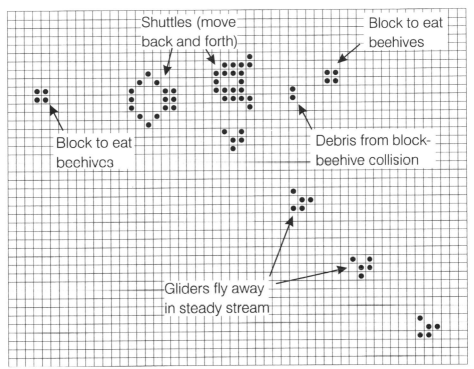

The Glider Gun setup. Objects have to be placed precisely so debris from colliding objects fades away. An endless stream of gliders moves toward the lower right. (Courtesy of Katherine Macfarlane)

through a series of transformations that resulted in the whole object moving one space diagonally on the grid. This object became known as a glider. The glider, in theory, might move forever.

Conway believed that if a continually growing Life pattern could be designed, it would be a major step toward showing the truth of von Neumann's ideas about living machines. Conway challenged the readers of Martin Gardner's column on mathematical games in *Scientific American* to demonstrate such a growing Life pattern.

One reader of this column, William Gosper, took up Conway's challenge. Gosper, a top computer expert at the Massachusetts Institute of Technology's artificial intelligence laboratory, had already become hooked on the Game of Life, running thousands of generations of patterns on the lab's computers. Gosper and his colleagues went to work, and in a month they had come up with a "glider gun," a pattern that produced and ejected one glider after another. Unfortunately, the gliders eventually collided with other objects or created objects that destroyed the gun. By placing appropriate objects to "kill" stray fragments, Gosper was finally able to create a glider gun setup that amounted to a perpetually growing Life pattern.

Eventually, Gosper was able to show that a large, complex Life pattern could be actually used as a computer, performing additions. While still nowhere as complicated as von Neumann's machine, the seemingly simple Game of Life had demonstrated a new field of cellular automation or—as it soon came to be called—"artificial life."

The new field expanded during the 1980s and later included many other "games" that modeled such things as genetics, the role of DNA in carrying information between generations of living things, and the process of evolution and natural selection. Ideas from cellular automation have been used by biologists to explain the behavior of flocks of birds.

Conway continues to explore new frontiers in mathematics. In recent years, he's been trying to figure out the best way to pack a bunch of spheres into a particular space—in eight dimensions. It turns out that this seemingly abstract problem has practical uses in encoding computer data in eight-bit chunks. The eight data bits can be represented by one point in the eight-dimensional universe, given in terms of the center of the nearest sphere. Conway says, "I find it lovely that this purely geometrical thing that I'm interested in is actually useful to quite practical people." But as Chern found out, the most abstract sorts of mathematics often turn out to be mirrors of the way nature works.

Chronology

December 26, 1937	John H. Conway born in Liverpool, England
1950s	John von Neumann and Stanislaw Ulam do early work on "cellular automata"
1959	Conway gets B.A. from University of Cambridge
1962	earns doctoral degree; becomes lecturer at Cambridge
1970	introduces "Game of Life"
1981	becomes a fellow of the Royal Society
1985–	serves as John von Neumann Professor of Mathematics at Princeton University
1987	wins IEEE award for outstanding paper and Polya Prize of the London Mathematical Society

Further Reading

Albers, Donald J. "Conway: Talking a Good Game." *Math Horizons* (Spring 1994): 6–9. A good introduction to Conway's approach to mathematics; includes a sidebar on the Game of Life.

———, and G. L. Alexanderson, eds. *Mathematical People: Profiles and Interviews*. Chicago: Contemporary Books, 1985. Has a chapter on John H. Conway.

Kolata, Gina. "John Conway: At Home in the Elusive World of Mathematics." *New York Times,* Oct. 12, 1993, pp. C1, C10. Interview where Conway describes how he explores mathematics.

Poundstone, William. *The Recursive Universe: Cosmic Complexity and the Limits of Scientific Knowledge*. New York: William

Morrow, 1985. Despite its formidable title, this book includes a good introduction to Conway's Game of Life for beginners.

Prata, Stephen. *Artificial Life Playhouse*. Corte Madera, California: Waite Group Press, 1993. This book describes eight different computer programs (including Conway's Game of Life and simulations of evolution); includes ready-to-run software.

Index

Boldface numbers indicate main headings.
Italic numbers indicate illustrations.